How to Get Off the FAST TRACK ▶ and Live a Life Money Can't Buy

How to Get Off
the *FAST TRACK* ▶
and Live a Life
Money
Can't Buy

M. M. Kirsch

Lowell House
Los Angeles
CONTEMPORARY BOOKS
Chicago

Library of Congress Cataloging-in-Publication Data

Kirsch, M. M., 1954–
    How to get off the fast track—and live a life
money can't buy / by M.M. Kirsch.
    p. cm.
    ISBN 0-929923-41-3 : $19.95
    1. Quality of work life—United States—Case
studies. 2. Quality of life—United States—Case
studies. 3. Career changes—United States—Case
studies. 4. Vocational interests—United States—
Case studies. I. Title.
    HD6957.U6K57 1991   91-3745
    650.1—dc20   CIP

Publisher: JACK ARTENSTEIN

Vice-President/Editor-in-Chief: JANICE GALLAGHER

Director of Marketing: ELIZABETH DUELL WOOD

Design: MIKE YAZZOLINO

Manufactured in the United States of America
10   9   8   7   6   5   4   3   2   1

TO TODD AND RILEY

I'd like to thank Janice Gallagher at Lowell House for her patience. Special thanks to Mary Nadler, my editor, who came into the project at the eleventh hour and made it happen. And a final thank-you to all of the "mavericks" out there who so generously shared their adventures.

Contents

Introduction

Our panic about where our lives were going first began in 1982, on a beautiful, sunshiny Thanksgiving Day, as my husband Todd and I walked our dog around the block in West Hollywood.

We were renting one of the old Charlie Chaplin bungalows, built to accommodate visiting movie stars back in the 1930s. It was one of the more charming places to live in the city—walking distance from ethnic restaurants, ice cream parlors, rare book and record stores, comedy theaters, you name it. We had been living there since 1976.

Todd was a successful commercial photographer, shooting for both American and Japanese clients. I owned my own commercial agency and wrote on the side. We had virtually no responsibilities beyond doing our work, paying our bills, and taking care of Tucson, our golden retriever. Perhaps it was walking around the block for the umpteenth time with a dog who belonged in the country that triggered our realization that we were really going nowhere. We were working hard and enjoying successful careers, yet something was missing. Because we had no commitments, we had no real direction or purpose to our lives. Todd stopped abruptly on the sidewalk and said, "If we don't change now, we'll be doing the same thing in 10 years."

We talked for a long time about what we wanted to do for work, where we wanted to be in 10 years, and what we both wanted and didn't want from life. Todd wanted to do less photography and more designing of houses. I wanted more time to write. We were afraid of becoming dependent on any one employer or on the whims of the marketplace—we had witnessed too many people fired from jobs after years of dedication. We missed our families, and we missed the country. We wanted our own home. We wanted children. The carefree lifestyle we lived offered little solace compared to what we truly wanted.

We resolved to change our life and to commit to a 10-year plan to make happen what we wanted to have happen. Our plan evolved in three stages and focused on a change in lifestyle and the use of real estate and "sweat equity."

We took our first step one weekend when we went for a picnic in the San Bernardino National Forest. Todd and I came across a ramshackle cabin in the woods for sale. We stepped inside to a scene out of *David Copperfield*—cobwebs hung three feet from the ceiling, a trapdoor leading to the upstairs bedroom and bath hadn't been opened in years, and newspapers provided the only insulation. We made an offer and bought the place! It was the first big risk of our 10-year plan.

The second stage of our plan involved driving across the western United States during vacations in search of the place we would eventually move to. Nothing satisfied our criteria until we finally discovered an old farm on a lake 10 miles outside of Rhinelander, Wisconsin, where I grew up. We drove down a dirt road beneath a canopy of trees, then out onto a spectacular meadow of wildflowers at the end of which was a small farmhouse, a magnificent barn from the early 1900s, and a beautiful lake with white birch and white pine along the shore line. Without speaking a word, Todd and I knew this was where we wanted to live. We were barely able to afford the down payment. It was the second major risk in our 10-year plan. Before we even knew how we were going to leave the city, we owned the place we would move to!

The final stage of our plan involved selling the cabin we had first purchased and which Todd had renovated, and using the money to buy raw land in the Hollywood Hills. Todd designed and built a house there that will give us the equity we need to make the final transition to our new home in Wisconsin. Before we began building in Hollywood, we purchased a Victorian home in Rhinelander with a very small down payment. During vacations, Todd converted it into a duplex, which will give us rental income when we move.

As for work, over the years we have both developed a variety of job skills that will allow us to earn income in several different ways.

Meanwhile, in spring 1990 we had our first child, a daughter.

Throughout this period, we couldn't find a useful book on the subject of making such a transition. Books on the subject were either pure psychology or "back-to-the-land" homestead manuals, neither of which suited our purpose. Over the years, the best advice we got came from people who were actually making the move off the fast track and pursuing their dreams. The chance to learn from their mistakes and successes has helped us to speed up our own departure.

When we move to our farm outside of Rhinelander, we will have lived in Los Angeles for 16 years. At various points during that time, we have worked fast-track careers, commuted from the country, and operated four businesses out of our home. We have experienced the best and worst of city living.

We would not be moving to the country to settle if we had not taken advantage of the opportunities that have come our way in the city. We are not running from the fast track or from the city, but looking forward to happily continuing our lives in a quieter, simpler place that is more in harmony with our vision of the good life.

I have written this book to share what we have learned along the way, both from our own experiences and from the experiences of others. This is not a business-oriented book, telling you how to find a job, how to start a business, how to buy the best real estate, how to invest your money and retire fat and happy, and so on. Nor is this a book about homesteading, going back to the land, or practicing an ascetic life. What I am offering instead is a way for you to harness your dreams to a practical plan, one that is tailor-made to your special circumstances and that will allow you to achieve your vision of the good life—doing what you want to do, and living where you want to live. The book will first help you to determine whether you are cut out to get out, and it will then take you step by step through the process of getting off the fast track and into your new life.

The people whose stories appear in this book are all very real. It is remarkable how much in common they have, how many similar characteristics they share. I was amazed at how easy it was to develop a profile of what I call the "maverick"—the successful ex–fast-tracker. In the pages that follow, you will meet these mavericks. You'll find out why they opted to get off the fast track, and how they did it.

Reading the stories of successful ex–fast-trackers from across the country who share their firsthand experiences and their insights may be the next best thing to being there. But in the end, the idea is for you to be there—wherever, and whatever, you choose "there" to be.

1

You may have a success in life, but then just think of it—what kind of life was it? What good was it—you've never done the thing you wanted to do in all your life . . . go where your body and soul want to go. When you have the feeling, then stay with it, and don't let anyone throw you off.

JOSEPH CAMPBELL
The Power of Myth

Who Gets Out, and Why

ACCOUNTANT TURNED CHRISTMAS-TREE FARMER

Bruce Niedermeier has been shaping Christmas trees all day. He started early this morning and it's now 4:30. Bruce owns a 251-acre Christmas-tree farm and has a quarter million white pine, balsam, spruce, Scotch pine, and frazier pine planted. He lives in a 1901 farmhouse that he helped his father restore. He eats every meal with his artist wife and their two young children.

Five years ago, Bruce was a marketing expert and computer whiz at a Big Eight accounting firm in Houston. He was working as many as 60 hours a week including Saturdays. He had a stiff mortgage to pay, a long commute to work, and often ate dinner at the office. His wife, Lori, was attending classes full time.

One fine April day, they decided to pack up their belongings and head for Wild Rose, Wisconsin, where Bruce hoped to make a go of it as a Christmas-tree farmer taking over his father's retirement project.

The main reason I left the firm in Houston was that things just didn't feel right. I'd been promoted, I was making lots of money, and I had a job I was very good at. But it just wasn't satisfying, and I wasn't happy with all the business politics.

Lori and I had talked about getting out for about six months, and when April rolled around, we did it even though we couldn't sell our house because of the depressed real estate market. We had to continue paying the mortgage for a number of months after we moved and we finally had to sell at a loss.

This farm was Dad's retirement project. He'd started planting trees 10 years ago and now he wanted out of the farm operation because it had gotten too big for him.

I had lined up a job as an assistant to the vice-chancellor at the university near here so I'd have some income that first year. I supplement the farm income doing computer consulting. I do a lot of it for other growers, and I learn from their mistakes.

My first year here I volunteered for the Wisconsin Christmas Tree Producers Association and became editor for the paper. It was the perfect opportunity to meet everyone and get to know the business. I turned a six-page mimeograph into a 32-page glossy. I worked for free and shared my marketing skills so everyone could profit. The rewards for me were more than double. I greatly improved my writing skills, and I earned the trust and respect of the other growers.

It has taken me 4 years to become an expert at this job. Today, we could sell twice the number of trees if we had them to sell. In 5 years, the farm equipment will be paid off. In 10, I'll probably be earning what I would have earned if I'd stayed in Houston and become a partner at the firm!

That's not to say, of course, that I don't face risks. For instance, in 1987 I lost every balsam, white pine, spruce, and frazier that I planted; the heat just burned them up. That means nine years down the line, it's going to hurt me. But that's all part of the challenge.

The important thing is that the quality of life is higher for us here. We don't miss the fancy cars and the expensive clothes, meals, and entertainment. Lori and I drive into town to see a movie and have some Chinese food. We don't have any traffic, yet there is a shopping mall an hour away.

I know everybody here. There's nothing like walking into a restaurant on a cold snowy morning, ordering a cup of hot coffee, stamping your feet, slapping the cold off your arms, blowing your nose—and everybody is agreeing with you that hell yes its cold out there and they all call you by name.

We go bowling. We have the best Friday night fish fries. We even have season tickets to the theater at the university in Stevens Point! We couldn't be happier.

THE EX–FAST-TRACKERS

A banker and her husband, a former car salesman, quit their careers to start an international cycle-touring company.

A successful Manhattan leather-goods manufacturer liquidates, moves upstate, and becomes a goat farmer producing French-style goat cheese.

A Wall Street stockbroker walks away from a six-figure salary so he can manage a short-of-cash riding stable in Tucson.

A successful New York City businesswoman decides she wants out, buys property in New Mexico, and opens a bed-and-breakfast inn.

A graphic designer and his wife, both filmmakers, forfeit lucrative businesses in San Francisco and move to a remote rural area in California. They start a business handcrafting beautiful books using nineteenth-century methods.

These sudden, seemingly unpredictable changes in career and lifestyle are triggered by changes in the perception of what it means to live "the good life." The excesses of consumerism and careerism have taken their toll. Men and women of all ages are walking away from prestigious, highly successful careers to enter lifestyles in which they earn only a fraction of their previous incomes.

These people tell tales of high risk, blind faith, tenacity, and uncertain futures, combined with adventure and extraordinary gumption. They talk about living balanced lives, working at what they love to do, and finding time for and appreciating the simpler joys in life. They tell of community involvement and individual responsibility, of practicing an ethical philosophy that improves society as a whole.

For these ex–fast-trackers (whom we'll call ex-FTers, for convenience), the good life began with a personal vision of happiness. Their individual interests, skills, and family relationships, combined with a clear focus on their innermost values and a code of ethics, helped define this vision. Though they talk about the sacrifices, the lack of money, the unstinting commitment, they also talk about a deeper, more abiding, peaceful state of mind—happiness, if you will.

If you have picked up this book, chances are you have felt a similar dissatisfaction with your life. Perhaps you aren't sure what's missing. Do you yearn to "settle down," to make a stronger commitment to family and friends? Are you in search of more meaningful work? Do you love your work but need a change of environment? Do you feel a strong urge to simplify your life? One place to start in answering these questions is to ask, "How did I get on the fast track, and why am I still here?"

THE LURE OF THE FAST TRACK

For some, the lure of the fast track is its promise of financial security, freedom to travel, unlimited opportunity, and the ease to spend money without feelings of guilt or worry about old age and retirement. For others, the fast track offers a chance to exploit their best talents as deal makers, salespeople, computer whizzes, organizers, debaters, administrators, and a host of other skills. There are those who see the fast track as a chance to do what their parents couldn't—own a second home, send their children to private schools, vacation in the Caribbean. For many, then, the fast track has given them a feeling of self-worth and rewarded them with a brand of success they find satisfying.

For others, however, the fast track leads down a road without purpose. Their goals bring them financial success but not peace of mind. How did they become so misdirected? What did they find so attractive, so intoxicating about the fast track? Was it someone else's idea of the successful career, the successful lifestyle? Do they really want to be stockbrokers, systems analysts, attorneys, accountants, advertising directors, executives punching time clocks 70 hours a week? Did they become professionals—doctors, lawyers, architects, designers— simply to earn a lot of money? Are they looking for security? Are these careers truly fulfilling? Do they offer a sense of accomplishment? Are they a chance to practice personal skills and talents? Are they a true reflection of the person?

What does it mean to say you are on the fast track? Many fast-trackers earn more than $50,000 a year. (Earnings are relative to the size of the city you work in. To be a fast-tracker in New York City, you most likely earn more than $100,000.) Many work approximately 60 hours a week and are often "on-call" for the weekend. Many fast-trackers work for someone other than themselves (an employer who controls much of their time). Many live and work in a city.

Working Girl, Manhattan, and *Pretty Woman* are three popular motion pictures that capture the seductive aspects of the fast track, its promise of glamour, prestige, self-assurance, power. It came dressed by Armani, driven by Ferrari, and fed with nouvelle cuisine. Once you stepped on, you could swagger all the way to the bank. Your ticket to the fast track was a willingness to work the hardest at the jobs that paid the most. In our eagerness to "make it," however, many of us forgot to question the target. The frenetic pace dimmed our sensibilities.

It is not difficult to understand why so many bought into a version of success that promised little in the way of self-worth and accomplishment. Television, magazines, and billboards on every corner work to convince us that making money is the single road to success. But the media is only partially to blame. Religious and intellectual traditions have been replaced by short-order entertainment and comforts that do nothing to feed the soul.

At home and in much of our education, we most likely were offered little discussion of the real nature of humanity and the world. Young people thus are left with little to guide them concerning the possibilities of their lives. Academic vocationalism long ago replaced the liberal education meant to give students the means to examine who they are and appraise their unique potentials. The works of the great writers have been shelved in favor of business, engineering, and science texts that can assure one of a secure livelihood, making lots of money.

In 1984, more than twice as many undergraduates earned business degrees as in 1971. A survey of more than 200,000 college freshmen in 1987 conducted by the American Council on Education found that 76% felt it essential to be very well off financially.

Too often, young adults go to college to learn how to make money, not to question and learn about themselves and the world they live in. The notion of entering the university in order to develop a philosophy of life strikes many as absurd, as a waste of time. What can philosophy teach that will enhance their success in the ever more competitive job market?

Students graduate with a degree that will get them a job, and they believe that their education is complete. This "job" is what they must do. Students not locked into instant careers are frequently pitied rather than admired. As Theodore Roszak wrote in *The Making of a Counter Culture*, "This now-or-never pressure is one of the worst tyrannies of the system; it denies us the freedom to experiment, to fail, to turn back, to begin again—if necessary, to start a second career, to launch a new life."

Our ignoble middle-class mentality long ago substituted a money standard for the more worthy standards of the ancient Greeks, who valued intellectual curiosity, an appreciation for beauty, the need to communicate and understand one another, and a profound respect for the world around them.

In *The Hunger for More*, Lawrence Shames describes the brand of success that has evolved from this money standard as having "lost its reference to accomplishment, to high intent . . . recognized only in terms of its reward. Ambition, which rightly has to do with finding balance and scope for all of one's abilities, [is] whittled down to mean getting on a career track. Taste and quality, much invoked in the eighties, [are] trivialized to mean largely what things cost and where they [can] be bought."

Thus, we find 55-year-old businesspeople, 42-year-old attorneys, and 33-year-old Wall Street traders suddenly asking, "Is that all there is?" They make more money than they ever imagined, live more comfortably than they ever hoped to, and enjoy the respect and admiration that goes with "making it." Yet the deep thirst for something else, something that is missing in their lives, drives them to their psychotherapists, triggers mid-life crises, and dissolves marriages.

Some haven't a clue where to look to fill this void. When they are advised to look within themselves, they see the reflection of their outer pursuits and goals. When they attempt to "feel" their way to happiness, they get swindled by the popular guru of the day. They have no foundation of beliefs or values to guide them. Their resource material is limited to popular magazines, the evening news, and the latest in self-help books, cassettes, and videos. They are unhappy, nagged by feelings of emptiness, boredom, and dwindling self-esteem. They see themselves in striking contrast to others—some on the fast track, some living much simpler lives, but individuals who have achieved contentment and find their work and the way they live their lives completely satisfying.

Such individuals have an enviable attitude that says, "If it doesn't get any better than this, that's perfectly all right with me." These are people who struggled to acquire a knowledge of the world and the role they might play in the scheme of things, a role developed from the exercise of their unique talents and skills. Those who chose the fast track and did so for better reasons than just to make money. *They love what they do and feel a genuine sense of accomplishment. They keep their work, their leisure, and their love relationships in balance.*

In contrast is the engineer, the broker, the commercial designer, the advertising executive, the lawyer, the physician, the businessperson—who does what he or she does merely to afford a six-figure standard of living and live the contemporary definition of success. Such people derive little inner satisfaction from the work they do. What they discover is that earning lots of money, working long hours, and living a lavish lifestyle do not guarantee *peace of mind, loving relationships, or a deep sense of personal worth*. These are the things that are missing in their lives.

FILLING THE VOID

To change your life and leave the fast track behind, you will first need to identify clearly what you do and do not want out of life in order to discover what is missing now. Chapter 2 will help you determine whether getting off the fast track completely is the answer for you; chapter 3 will help you develop a personal vision of happiness that allows you to set up objectives directed at achieving that vision.

Ex-FTers who successfully made the transition considered the quest more a search for a state of mind, for a well-ordered inner harmony that comes from choosing to live with a strong sense of purpose and control of one's destiny. For them, it involved making an emotional and intellectual lifetime commitment to a better quality of life. Such a commitment entailed a responsibility that guaranteed hard work, struggles, perseverance, sacrifices, discipline, and a lot less of the carefree attitude they were accustomed to in their more lucrative fast-track days of dining out, traveling at will, and generally spending "disposable income."

Getting married, raising children, developing one's talents, nurturing relationships, and participating in the community are the kind of commitments that involve profound changes in day-to-day life. They take time and energy—commodities in short supply if you run on the fast track. Frank Rhodes, president of Cornell, addressed this phenomenon in his 1990 commencement address at Caltech:

> Commitment to anything beyond one's immediate sphere was anathema just a few years ago, when much of daily life seemed focused on avoiding commitments of any kind. Even marriage and family life were to be put off as long as possible, if not permanently, because of the potentially constraining commitments they might entail. It was a simpler life, in some ways, but one that was

ultimately unfulfilling, for it is our commitments that give meaning and purpose to our lives. If the yuppies of the eighties have taught us anything, it is that life without commitment is superficial and unsatisfying, that a triumphant career is not enough. "Hollow men and moral nomads" reap not fulfillment, but futility.

An astonishing number of today's fast-trackers say they are ready and prepared to make commitments in order to fill the voids in their lives. They find themselves driven by a deep urge to take more responsibility for their lives, their relationships, and the world around them. Many, however, don't know where to begin. This book will show you how to get off the fast track and start living the life you long to live.

WHY GET OFF THE FAST TRACK?

High-salaried managers, dentists, interior designers, traders, lobbyists, commercial photographers, software technicians, PhDs, and hundreds of other professional and corporate types, ranging in age from their early twenties to their late fifties, give the same kinds of answers to why they are moving to Seattle, Washington; Cedar Rapids, Iowa; Missoula, Montana; Madison, Wisconsin; Park City, Utah; and variety of other places.

They talk about having more time to work in the garden, to play catch with the kids, to sit down to a home-cooked meal. They talk about breathing cleaner air, paying off their mortgages, driving down country roads. They talk about not answering the phone every 10 minutes, having spontaneity in their lives, working at hobbies they never had time for before. They talk about living in safer neighborhoods, sending their kids to better schools, and feeling a greater sense of community. They talk about participating in their communities and contributing to society. Many get off the fast track to live their lifelong dreams.

Kirsten Dixon wrote in *Harrowsmith* (March, 1988) about why she and her husband left the fast track and started a fishing lodge business for vacationing outdoorsmen in Alaska's wilderness.

> My husband Carl and I had been living in Anchorage, Alaska, in the typical professional mode. I was a nurse and he was an audiologist. . . . My job had odd hours, and Carl's involved quite a bit of traveling to villages all over Alaska. We hardly ever saw each

other, and when we did, I always had a feeling hanging over my head that soon we would have to leave each other again. We felt that we were being robbed of time. We had a nice home and nice things, but no time to enjoy them. After we had our first daughter, Carly, and she began spending her early life at a day-care center, we decided enough was enough. . . . Carl's easy way with people and love of the outdoors and my interests in cooking and gardening seemed to be a perfect combination for running a fishing lodge. We found a spot perfect for us, 70 air miles northwest of Anchorage. It's a 45-minute flight by "air taxi." We quit our jobs, sold out of Anchorage, and flew out to our new life on the river.

KIRSTEN AND CARL DIXON
Fishing Lodge Owners
Lake Creek, Alaska

Some choose to leave the fast track in order to spend more time with family and friends. They may do this by working out of their homes, starting their own businesses, or finding jobs that let them go home at 5 o'clock and give them the weekends off.

I don't work on the weekends anymore. We pack up our family and go to the mountains. Friday afternoons I take piano lessons, and my wife spends a lot of her time painting. There was a lot of money to be made in Los Angeles in the real estate market. Because I was also a professional musician there was always the possibility, the dream, of writing that hit song—but it doesn't mean much in the long run. We live a wonderful life here, and we're all very happy.

PETER PARNEGG
Real Estate Broker
Albuquerque, New Mexico

Jon Goodson used to work long hours as a dairy nutritionist for an animal-feed company in Delaware, Ohio. He and his wife Meg moved their family to remote Kellys Island, Ohio. Jon now uses his personal computer to continue his career from his home on a consultant basis, spending a few days a week working for his former employer and occasionally commuting to the mainland. During the summer months, the Goodsons operate a restaurant they purchased with their savings. Jon speaks of the "quality" time he can now spend with his kids: "Before, I'd get home in time to kiss the kids good night.

Now, I'm here when they leave for school, and I'm here when they get home" (*USA Weekend*, September 14, 1990).

For some, the main reason to leave their fast-track careers is to gain more control over their time. Bill Rauch was the press secretary for the mayor of New York City and frequently put in 80-hour workweeks. Today, he runs a small-town newspaper in Beaufort, South Carolina, which he likes to call "slow country." His wife Jennifer, a former lobbyist in New York, operates a historic-preservation business out of their home and writes a weekly column for the local newspaper. An article in *USA Weekend* described their new lifestyle: "Instead of harried commutes and exhausting workweeks, the Rauches have the time and energy for neighborhood barbecues and for reviving a once-overgrown garden." Switching to small-town life also gives them more time with their two young children who can now play safely outdoors.

Have you ever dreamed of running a small coffee shop, a bookstore, a small country business in one of the more beautiful areas of the country? Norman and Claire Weiss had a rich lifestyle in New York and Los Angeles, where Norman worked in the entertainment industry. They gave it up to become the proprietors of Dolly's Books Etc., a bookstore in the ski-resort town of Park City, Utah. Of the old life, Norman says,

> My feet never touched the ground. I'd get picked up in a limo, driven right to the plane, and there'd be another limo on the other end. It started boring me to tears and I just didn't want to do it anymore. . . . The whole idea is to . . . live a simple, unencumbered life. (*Los Angeles Times*, December 2, 1990)

Some choose to get off the fast track because their employer is too demanding. Mike Powers was one of the original computer whiz kids. He loved his work but hated working for a corporation. At one time he had four offices across the United States.

> I was a computer center operations manager. I have a bachelor's degree from Carnegie-Mellon and a master's from MIT. I worked for Pfizer's for 17 years. I got out because the corporate mentality hammered me. You are expected to work countless hours and be on call 24 hours a day, and that includes Christmas Eve. They'd have a systems breakdown and be calling me on Christmas Eve to go fix things. My job was to get the next poor guy down the line out of his home, and I just wouldn't do that to somebody.

Today, I'm very happy to be milking cows and selling auto parts. I have free time now that I never had before. I can do something on the spur of the moment that I could never do before. My entire life was doing computer business. Now I can sleep through the night, and I don't have to answer the phone.

MIKE POWERS
Auto Parts Salesman, Dairy Farmer
Norwich, Connecticut

Paul Terhorst, author of *Cashing In on the American Dream*, describes the inner restlessness that finally drove him to quit his job.

After 12 years of work I had a good income and a full complement of executive trappings. I met with big people about big deals involving big bucks. But as the song in *A Chorus Line* goes, "That ain't it, kid." I wasn't getting many jollies at the office. . . . The inner need was like a seismic fissure deep in the rock under a ski run. Resort owners treat the fissure by dynamiting the mountain. . . . The alternative—to do nothing—may work for a while. But sooner or later there'll be an avalanche and almost certain disaster. When you reach the anxiety of mid-life plateau, you're the fissure in the rock. You can blast yourself into a new mountain. Or you can suffocate in the crushing avalanche of middle management, hoping for the vaguely defined big break somewhere down the line.

Robin Ogden and her husband moved to the Midwest from Los Angeles to live a more traditional lifestyle.

The violence, the smog, the congestion in Los Angeles . . . most important, I wanted out because of our four-year-old daughter. I wanted to be able to take her to the park without having to drive there. We wanted to buy a home with a front yard for our daughter to play in.

ROBIN OGDEN
Artist Representative
Minneapolis, Minnesota

Others, such as Jody Rush, begin to think life is passing them by.

I wanted out of Washington, D.C., mainly because of burnout. I was traveling 90% of the time. Home wasn't really home for me. I met a fella at the airport in Memphis when our plane had a five-hour layover. He offered me a job in Austin, Texas! I had done some work in the oil field just out of college and had made several friends in Texas, so I wasn't a stranger to the place. . . . Now that I'm here, I have found a home. I'm ready to settle in and raise a family.

JODY RUSH
Chamber of Commerce
Austin, Texas

An article in *Psychology Today* (November, 1989) talked about people who yearn to do more meaningful work. One, George Delaney, started his own company—the Delaney Design Group—after having worked for a large firm. He grew tired, he says, of "always gilding someone else's lily." Delaney reports that self-employment "is addictive in a number of ways—autonomy, skill integration, making and learning from your own mistakes. It's a full-blown encounter with risk, and with your ability to create products or services of real worth." He discovered that his work "instilled a sense of meaning in my life that I never was able to feel before. You have to be good to survive, and my little business afforded me a sense of discovering what high quality in work meant. I'd like my two young sons to one day know who their dad is through my work, not through what I bought or earned." This feeling of accomplishment and self-worth gained from one's work is a key ingredient in the formula for making a successful transition off the fast track.

Let's meet a few more ex-FTers.

SALESMAN AND BANKER TURNED CYCLISTS

Larry Barnes grew up in Los Angeles. He spent six years in the service, then returned to Los Angeles and worked as a sales rep for automotive manufacturers wholesaling to dealerships. Mary Jane Barnes grew up in Eastern Canada. She moved to Western Canada at a time of great prosperity in the oil business and enjoyed a promising career in banking.

Larry: After I was in the Coast Guard I discovered there was another life outside the big city. I worked hard in Los Angeles for about three years making great money when I decided to change my focus. I wanted to be guided not by career but by where I would most enjoy living. I decided first to find a place where I wanted to live and then figure out how to make a living there.

I had a variety of job skills from time spent in the Coast Guard. I was a boat rigger and a "damage control man," which includes being a welder, a pipefitter, and a carpenter.

I decided to move to Lake Tahoe. I worked as a boat rigger first, then started selling boats. Before long I was able to start my own charter boat company. After four years I sold the business.

I had a feeling of wanderlust again, got on my bike and road to Canada, where I discovered Banff while I was riding through the Rocky Mountains. It was beautiful, and perfectly suited to bicycle touring, which was a hobby of mine. Bicycle touring and bicycle racing were hobbies from when I was young.

In 1977, I used the capital from the sale of my charter boat business and, along with my wife Mary Jane, started a bike touring business near Banff called "Rocky Mountain Cycle Tours." Both my wife and I were firm believers that you should do what you want to do, not what is forced on you. The extra money earned staying on the fast track is what you substitute for living the life-style you really want.

When Mary Jane's banking career brought her to this area, she fell in love with the place. We had talked about starting up this hobby business, and we decided to do it. Mary Jane used her economic and organizational skills to help get the business going. She elected not to continue her banking career and worked pretty much full time on our business, occasionally supplementing our income doing part-time travel desk work.

I worked five years as a carpenter to make ends meet. I'd advise anyone wanting to do something similar to what we have done to hang in there because it takes a long time. It took us 10 years before our business made it on its own.

Originally, it was a short biking season, from June to September. We spent the off-season doing marketing, promotion, and advertising, which all cost money. Today, we work all four seasons. This winter we have bicycle tours in Hawaii, New Zealand, and Japan. In the summer we have tours in the Rocky Mountains and Western Canada. In the spring, it's Norway, Italy, and Germany. In the fall, we do tours in France and Germany. I travel on 90% of the tours. Our seven-year-old son usually goes along, and it's great fun for him.

I had some exposure to international travel while in the Coast Guard, but the key to our success is Mary Jane's experience and skills. She has excellent language skills and business acumen. I'm the operational manager of the equipment, and I take care of the technical and mechanical end of things. Combining our skills and experience, we make a pretty good business team.

One way our lives are different is that we don't wait for the weekend. We do a lot of outdoor recreation, including cross-country skiing, downhill skiing, and biking and sailing, and we do this during the week when we want to. We're also pretty involved with the community, especially since we bring a lot of business here. We had the Olympic venue for Nordic competition here, so we can take advantage of that.

I see only one possible drawback to what we do, and that is not having enough time to just stay home!

LARRY AND MARY JANE BARNES
Cycle Tour Operators
Canmore, Alberta, Canada

ADWOMAN/ARCHITECT TURNED INNKEEPER

Sue Smoot left New York City after spending several years in the advertising business and then earning a degree in architecture. On the brink of launching a career as an architect, she decided to pursue an old dream of hers—to run a bed-and-breakfast inn in a beautiful part of the country for a clientele with whom she could share breakfast and good conversation. Six months later, La Posada de Taos, a beautiful old adobe hacienda, was open for business in Taos, New Mexico.

I loved New York. It worked for me. It was just getting harder to love. I had always wanted to buy an inn, so I just up and decided to take a 6,000-mile trip across the country to pick the ideal location to start a bed and breakfast.

I traveled through Canada, Montana, Oregon, and Washington, and I finally decided on New Mexico. I started out in mid-June and in five weeks I had done my reconnaissance trip.

I had my criteria: I wanted a small place. I wanted a beautiful place. I wanted a melting pot of people, like New York—a good mix of people. I wanted a place that already attracted tourists. Finally, I would not live in air-conditioning. I once lived in Dallas and we went from heating to air-conditioning—hermetically sealed! I wouldn't ever do that again!

After I decided on Taos, I went back in October to do a feasibility report of facts and figures. I did a complete marketing report for myself. That's where I used my marketing background to work for me. Suddenly my research said GO! I knew I could do it.

I immediately sent out six letters to people I knew who were interested in buying my co-op in New York. The one who called me back got it. I packed up a Ryder truck with every possession I owned and drove with my daughter in three days from New York to Taos.

On October 20, we arrived. I had found a cute place for storage and things. Two weeks later my B & B place came on the market—it was the second property I had looked at! I closed on it November 6. On January 11 I was open for business.

All along I just knew it was going to work. I had enough in savings to hold me over for one year, just in case. I don't ever remember thinking I was taking a risk. You have to know what you can do and what you can't do. It is very instinctual. I did have one cliff-hanger, though, which was getting the loan to buy the place. I went to five different banks. All but the fifth bank turned me down and I got the loan one day before escrow closed.

This business is confining—you have to want to sit around and read and have your dinner interrupted by arrivals and know that it is a constant thing. But it is fun. Nobody's having more fun than I am!

SUE SMOOT
Innkeeper
Taos, New Mexico

EXECUTIVE TURNED FLY-MAKER

Poul Jorgensen was once a New York executive for a Swedish office-equipment company. He lived the fast-track cliché: a hefty salary, a beautiful home, two cars, an expensive lifestyle, and a job that demanded too many hours of work, too many years of stress, and too little time for himself and his family.

Today, Jorgensen is a celebrated figure in the fishing world. He has elevated the art of fly-tying to new heights, and collectors pay high prices and wait several months for a chance to purchase one of his remarkable creations. He has written several books on the subject that are best-sellers in the fishing field, and he travels throughout the world as a guest lecturer. A set of his framed flies was once given as a gift to Yugoslav President Tito from the Nixon White House.

Back in the early seventies, I was living in the fast lane. I was also a drunk. Then I lost everything—my wife, my kids, my property, my job. My life fell apart. A year later, I got into rehabilitation.

It was suggested to me then that getting back into my old job in the corporate community was not such a good idea. At that period of time I was concentrating on just staying alive. It was also suggested at the time I got sober that I start filling up the time I used to spend drinking with something else, like an old hobby. One of my old hobbies was tying flies for fishing, so I got back into that.

I started going to fishing shows and banquets. I was asked to tie flies, and then I started giving classes. At one of my demonstrations at a tackle show a publisher approached me and asked if I wanted to write a book on fly-tying, and I've written several since then.

I don't miss my former lifestyle at all. I had had enough. Back then, there was the new car every year, the new refrigerator. I live a much more modest life now. Your whole value system changes. I live by a river in the Catskill Mountains. I don't owe anybody a dime. People like to come visit me here. I've never been happier. I'm free to do whatever I want to do. I haven't had a drink in 20 years, and I still go to AA meetings every week. I don't take on anything now that might be detrimental to my health. I'm not a crusader—I just live life differently now.

The best advice I can give is to tell you this little story. A fellow who was writing an article about me for the *Wall Street Journal* came here to visit for a couple of days, and he told me how envious he was of my situation. He lived in New Jersey and hated the drive back and forth to the city. I told him he could do the same thing I was doing, but he said he couldn't quit his job working for the newspaper because he had kids in school, a mortgage to pay, and car payments. But I put the idea in his head, and he was really listening.

Well, six months later he called me up and said that he'd done it! He'd quit the paper and was off the racetrack. He was now editor-in-chief of his local newspaper. He works three days a week and goes fishing. He still lives in the same house and pays his bills.

If you're not happy with the way things are, then just get out. You can do it if you put your mind to it.

POUL JORGENSEN
Fly-Maker, Lecturer, Author
Roscoe, New York

COMMERCIAL ARTIST

Wayne Watford is a nationally known commercial illustrator who has worked in both the entertainment industry and commercial advertising.

I decided to move to Phoenix because my wife's family lives here. I had lived here a year and half before moving to Los Angeles for four years. We just didn't like it there. L.A. is scary; it's intimidating. I have son, and I didn't want to raise him in Los Angeles.

Living here is a lot easier because I don't have to deal with traffic. When I had to go for a meeting in L.A., it could take an hour and a half to get there and an hour and a half to get back. Afterward, I'd be so exhausted I didn't feel like working.

I work very little for the entertainment business now because they need such a fast turnaround. It used to be my primary source of income in Los Angeles. When I got a rep in St. Louis, I started getting work from all over the country.

We had a townhouse here before we moved to L.A., and we kept it when we moved. We lived in it when we first moved back, and then we bought a house. My son is happier here. We have family here, and he has all of his cousins to play with. When I go to the grocery store here, I can actually find a parking place in front of it! One of the big differences is in the cost of housing. I think it's also a little cheaper for food and things.

With the work that I do, I can live just about anywhere. The one thing I miss is my friends in the business back there. It was hard for me to make new friends when I moved, especially since I work all the time. My wife didn't have a hard time because she has three sisters here. Recently, I started playing basketball in the morning with some fellas. I think you just have to get involved. Just get something going, and you meet people.

I'm lucky that what I do lets me be here.

WAYNE WATFORD
Illustrator
Phoenix, Arizona

There are a variety of reasons why people leave the fast track. Some are looking to rekindle their spirits; some are looking for a cohesive social order to tighten the bonds of family and community; some hope to find more meaningful work. For some, such things as not having to lock doors and having the grocer know their first names become part of the criteria by which they measure success. The simple, yet crucial, awareness of what you are looking for will mean the difference between success and failure in your quest to find a better life. The solution to what is missing in your life may be as simple as refusing a promotion and as complicated as starting a new business in a different part of the country.

Do you wonder if there is a better life for you off the fast track? Are you wasting natural talents and skills because you have chosen a career that offers greater financial rewards? Do you feel that living in the country would improve the quality of your life? Are you eager to continue your education? Do you need more time for personal enlightenment? Is your work in balance with your family and personal needs? Do you long for a sense of accomplishment in your work?

Many hope for a combination of these things as they search for a quality of life emphasizing family values, civic responsibility, leisure time for personal enlightenment, and more meaningful work—a life that involves, as Robert Fulghum writes in *All I Really Need to Know I Learned in Kindergarten*, "learning some and thinking some and drawing and painting and singing and dancing and playing and working every day some."

As mentioned earlier, what ex-FTers seek is not a standard of living but a *state of mind, a well-ordered inner harmony that comes from choosing to live with a strong sense of purpose and control of one's destiny.* It is a state of mind that, as David Shi writes in *In Search of the Simple Life*, "preaches contentment and self-control and promises spontaneity and freedom."

If you are uncertain of whether you can make the commitment to step off the fast track, chapter 2 will help you discover whether you have what it takes—whether you fit the profile of the successful ex-FTer. And it will help you decide whether to take the first big step toward living your personal vision of the good life.

2

Try to keep your soul young and quivering
right up to old age, and to imagine right
up to the brink of death that life is only
beginning. I think that is the only way
to keep adding to one's talent, to one's
affections, and one's inner happiness.

GEORGE SAND

Are You Cut Out to Get Out?

DESIGNERS TURNED PUBLISHERS

Here in the woods, surrounded by oaks and Pacific madrones, Ponderosa and digger pines, by browsing deer and the ubiquitous tree frog whose stylized portrait serves as the press's emblem, the Robertsons have been making books since 1974. . . . The Yolla Bolly Press began publishing limited editions . . . books printed to last three hundred years or more on imported Italian paper, with handmade bindings, illustrated with original woodblocks and engravings. . . . Near their workshop—across the field—is the Robertsons' home; a meandering path leads to a rustic house for apprentices and another for the steady stream of writers, artists, and publishers who now find their way to Covelo, [California], and to a smaller barn being converted into an artist's studio. . . . A stone's throw from their workplace, the Robertsons have a garden, cut wood, [and] raise chickens. (*Horizon*, March, 1988)

My wife Carolyn and I [James] started out in commercial graphic design in the Bay Area. I was also teaching design at the time. Our work shifted after we became dissatisfied with the corporate scene. We wanted more interesting work, where input was not limited to design. We were also working in educational development and developed a film production company with a live-action film crew for publishers back East. Our educational materials were non-book print materials designed to accompany the films.

We were making a decent living, but we couldn't save, and we wanted to move to the country and buy our own place. We had been renting in Marin County, and we couldn't afford a place in the Bay Area.

When we started looking around for a piece of property, we had our criteria. We wanted to be within reasonable driving distance of the Bay Area—a half day. We wanted to be off any main arteries. We wanted to be in or near a small community.

We started looking around Mendocino County whenever we had free time. We did it on our own, without real estate agents. We knew what we wanted, and we knew we'd recognize it when we found it. When we saw these 40 acres in the Round Valley, we knew we wanted this place. It was two years before we moved to Covelo permanently. We had sort of planned on doing it in five years, but we couldn't wait!

We live in a very remote area near a community of 1,500. The local economy is chronically depressed—it's a timber and cattle town. We're accepted here, but we're still considered outsiders—we live six miles from town, we're in the publishing business, and we don't have a lot in common with the local people. Some people thought we were counterfeiters at first!

We didn't want to be isolated from the local community, though. Carolyn has been very active in the school district, because our child was in school there. I was involved with local land-use planning. Also, we opened a bookstore in town, where we also sell housewares. It's not a money-making venture—it can't be in a town this small—but it was a way for us to participate in the commerce of the community, a way for us to become a part of the community.

We made the transition in our work around the time we made our move with one educational project called the Brown Paper School Books. These books have provided us with a solid base, making it possible for us to do our limited-edition books. Each year we develop two to four trade books and do two or three limited-edition books, which we print here.

We are relatively free in all that we do, and we have enough success with our limited editions. We want to do what we believe in, and it's why we choose not to get any bigger, not to take on more projects, just to keep the machinery running. We don't ever want to be dependent on corporate clients. Our business is very hard work with long hours, yet we don't think of it that way because we enjoy it so much.

Our economic status has remained about the same. We still drink a good bottle of wine, we eat well, and when we go to the city we eat at fine restaurants. We have no mortgage. We paid that off in 15 years. But if you look at our actual income, we are probably below poverty level. It's why we could never do what we do in the city.

If I were to give advice to anyone—even though I don't like giving advice to someone I don't know—I would say that you have to have a good idea of what you want to do, of how you're going to make a living, before you move to the country. There isn't much of a selection of jobs in small rural areas like this. You have to bring your work with you or make it when you get there.

We work hard, and we produce something we believe in and that we are proud of. We live a good life.

DO YOU HAVE WHAT IT TAKES?

Getting off the fast track is an adventure reserved for the individual with a vision that comes from the heart. It is an adventure reserved for pioneer stock—the enterprising, the stalwart, the brave, the confident, the optimistic, and most important, the maverick. *Webster's New Collegiate Dictionary* defines a maverick as "an independent individual who refuses to conform with his group."

> If there is one piece of advice I'd offer to anyone considering getting out, it is that you have to be willing to take a big risk. It IS a big risk. You have to give up what you've got without knowing what you are going to get.
>
> ROBIN OGDEN
> *Minneapolis, Minnesota*

The two key ingredients that have enabled successful ex-FTers to get out are, first, a realistic sense of themselves (their aptitudes, talents, skills, and interests), and second, a clearly defined awareness of what they wanted from life (an idea of happiness unique to themselves and free of societal influences). In other words, to get off the fast track you need to know who you are and what you want.

In a recent Gallup poll of American adults, more than half of those polled said they would like to move to the country. Yet three-quarters of Americans still live in the city. What keeps them there? How many want to get out because they would like to find another way of life? What prevents them from making the move?

There may be several reasons why you're still on the fast track. Are you afraid of taking a big risk that jeopardizes your security? Do you hate the idea of starting over? Are you reluctant to walk away from a successful career after years of blood, sweat, and tears? Do you think your employer can take better care of you than you can yourself? Do you worry about what others would think?

You may have a variety of other reasons for why you can't seem to break free—problems that include confused priorities, inadequate information, indecision, uncertainty, a need for guidance, for strategy, perhaps even a challenge to your beliefs and values.

REASONS WHY YOU STAY ON THE FAST TRACK

Financial Concerns

You are afraid of experiencing a drop in income.

Your family is too dependent on your current income to maintain a certain lifestyle.

You are waiting to build more equity in your home.

You are too deeply in debt.

You worry that it would cost too much to relocate.

You find it difficult to estimate what you could earn if you stepped off the fast track.

Job Concerns

You are worried that you won't be able to find a job where you want to move.

You are uncertain about the type of work you want to do.

You are afraid that if you quit your current job you could never go back.

You are reluctant to walk away from a "successful" career.

FAMILY AND SOCIAL CONCERNS

You are afraid of moving to a new area and having to make new friends, start the kids in new schools, and begin a new social life.

You worry that a new area wouldn't offer enough cultural opportunities and might not be stimulating enough.

You have educational or religious needs that may not be met if you leave the city.

CONFUSED PRIORITIES

You are confused about the balance between your job, your family and friends, and your personal needs—unable to decide what is most important to you.

Where you want to live is equally as important as what you want to do, yet they conflict.

You are unclear about what is missing in your life.

FEAR OF TAKING RISKS

You are afraid of not knowing exactly what will happen once you step off the fast track.

You hate to take chances.

Your confidence is in direct proportion to the security you find in your work.

You can't remember the last time you took a risk.

The thought of striking out on your own frightens you.

LACK OF INFORMATION

You want out but don't know where to move.

You are unaware of the employment opportunities in the part of the country you want to move to.

You feel confused about where to begin to get off the fast track.

You are worried about what unknown sacrifices you may have to make.

If you recognize the reasons you remain on the fast track but are unable to resolve these issues, and if the urge to step off the fast track continues to haunt you, your biggest problem may be your inability to decide.

Getting off the fast track involves, first of all, a fundamental and profound decision to change your life. It is a decision that will affect where you live and what you do for work. It will affect the majority of people in your life—your family, your friends, your business associates, your neighbors, and the many acquaintances in your daily routine.

It is a decision that must be made with a strong conviction and a feeling that this is the only choice for you. It is a choice that will demand much hard work, perseverance, and staying power.

It is not a decision for those who are running away from their problems: in deciding to get off the fast track, you will meet more obstacles. Your quest to live the good life will challenge the status quo and much of what has made you feel secure.

The refusal to make a change holds many people back from realizing genuine happiness. Thousands complain of stress and treadmill workweeks. They say they want to spend more time with family and friends and to escape from the city's traffic, pollution, and crime. Yet they cannot bring themselves to make a decision. They fear the risk and they worry about what others will think. They procrastinate right into their graves.

Making the decision to get out is 99% of the journey. It requires self-analysis, a complete understanding of what one wants out of life, and a willingness to go the distance to make it a reality. It requires an internal shift, a conversion of sorts that has been likened to a spiritual awakening. It requires a profound confidence and belief in oneself.

There is always the possibility that you do not really want out. If asked what they most wish for, people may say a ranch in Montana, a farm in Iowa, a retreat in Hawaii. They fantasize about meadows, lakes, forests, the ocean. They say they want to read, to garden, to paint, to write. They say they want to raise a big family, build their own furniture, can their own peaches. The reason they don't do it now is because "in five years I'll have enough money." Five years down the line they are making more money and still talking about wanting to live the simple life.

In his book *Going Nowhere Fast*, Dr. Melvyn Kinder writes, "I conclude that we are becoming a nation of men and women who, in the quest for happiness, all too often fall short of achieving any kind of inner peace. Instead of life's journey being an exhilarating adv[en]ture into the unknown, for many of us it is a compulsive and tir[ing] trek, an exhausting journey where the next stop for replenishm[ent] never seems to arrive."

The fast-tracker who remains on the track year in and year o[ut] there because *he wants to be there*. He wouldn't give it up for al[l the] Walden Ponds in the world. If visions of moving to Marlboro cou[ntry] are your sole motivation, you might as well stay put.

HINTS THAT YOU BELONG ON THE FAST TRACK

You believe that lateral mobility would end your career.

You can't seem to earn enough income.

Your main plans for the future are financial.

You work late at the office out of habit (not because of work).

You believe the financial strategy that says, "leverage what you own."

You regret not having a law degree *and* an MBA.

You think leisure time is for the retired.

You prefer books on tape.

You are exasperated by buying groceries and cooking at home.

You prefer to hire help for most of your domestic chores.

When asked why you haven't taken action to get off the fast track, you have a number of excuses at hand:

I'll think about it after the first of the year.

I'm waiting until my career plateaus.

It will take a lot of study and planning.

I'd like to see others try it first.

I need to sleep on it.

I'm too busy right now.

I'll wait until the kids are older (or until I have kids).

Another year won't matter.

I'm making too much money to stop right now.

In *Think and Grow Rich,* Napoleon Hill discusses the psychological attributes of success and failure. Hill says that lack of persistence is "the real enemy which stands between you and noteworthy achievement." This lack of persistence is summed up as failure in 16 possible areas:

1. Failure to recognize and to define clearly exactly what one wants.

2. Procrastination, with or without cause.

3. Lack of interest in acquiring specialized knowledge.

4. Indecision, the habit of "passing the buck" on all occasions, instead of facing issues squarely.

5. The habit of relying upon alibis instead of creating definite plans for the solution of problems.

6. Self-satisfaction.

7. Indifference, usually reflected in one's readiness to compromise on all occasions, rather than meet opposition and fight it.

8. The habit of blaming others for one's mistakes, and accepting unfavorable circumstances as being unavoidable.

9. Weakness of desire, due to neglect in the choice of motives that impel action.

10. Willingness, even eagerness, to quit at the first sign of defeat.

11. Lack of organized plans, placed in writing where they may be analyzed.

12. The habit of neglecting to move on ideas, or to grasp opportunity when it presents itself.

13. Wishing instead of willing.

14. The habit of compromising instead of aiming. . . .

15. Searching for all the shortcuts . . . trying to get without giving a fair equivalent. . . .

16. Fear of criticism—failure to create plans and to put them into action because of what other people will think, do, or say.

WHAT IT TAKES TO GET OUT

Getting out requires strong motivation to make a major change in one's life. It is not an escape from problems, but a search for peace of mind and contentment.

Many ex-FTers were successful professionals who recognized their special talents and believed that they could be putting those talents to better use.

> It is your own conviction which compels you; . . . choice compels choice.
>
> EPICTETUS

Ruby Beale, 40, left 60-hour workweeks and constant business travel at her fast-track career in Boston to work as an assistant professor at the University of Michigan and do part-time consulting work.

Neil Laning, 44, a successful divorce attorney in Chicago, believes that he will find more joy in his life by switching his practice to business and real estate law in a small town in central Tennessee and participating in local community activities.

Anthony Stevens, 41, a Harvard MBA, quit his career as a banker in Washington, D.C. to take up organic farming in West Virginia.

The urge to get out is motivated by a personal desire to become the best one can be.

SELF-EVALUATION: ARE YOU CUT OUT TO GET OUT?

On a separate sheet of paper, write the numbers 1–50, and answer the following questions with *Yes, No,* or *Not Sure.*

1. Have you ever bartered your skills or talents for payment other than money?

2. Do yo feel confident that you are an expert in your field of work?

3. Have you ever worked two jobs at one time?

4. Would you call yourself noncommittal, with no particular set values?

5. Do you take risks easily in your personal life?

6. Do you take risks easily in your professional life?

7. Would you find more security working full-time for an employer rather than part-time for yourself?

8. Do you ever think about what you will be doing in five years?

9. Does it bother you what others think about you?

10. Do you think you could do a better job if you were the boss?

11. Do you spend a lot of time on hobbies or projects outside of your regular job?

12. Do you think often about changing careers?

13. Does the idea of working more for the money than for personal satisfaction bother you?

14. Do you feel yourself being confused and unhappy?

15. Are you pessimistic about the future?

16. Do you prefer to stay home on the weekends?

17. Have you made many difficult decisions that have dramatically changed your life?

18. Do you prolong making decisions rather than deciding things quickly?

19. Do you think you have already faced most of the major challenges of your life?

20. Do you consult associates, family, and friends before making major decisions?

21. Do you worry about losing business contacts you now have?

22. Do you usually do something you enjoy every day?

23. Do you welcome constructive criticism?

24. Are you reluctant to make changes in your social life, such as seeking out new friends and joining new organizations?

25. Are you always looking for ways to improve the work you do?

26. Are you currently or have you recently moonlighted—earned extra income doing work different from what you do in your regular job?

27. Do you find it difficult to make new friends?

28. Do you prefer to eat out instead of cooking at home?

29. Do you feel a sense of accomplishment in the work you are now doing?

30. Do you have job skills or talents that you currently don't use but would like to?

31. Have you initiated projects at work without the advice or recommendations of others?

32. Do you consider yourself relatively self-sufficient (home repairs, accounting, chores, and the like)?

33. Do you often laugh and take it in stride when things go wrong?

34. When you fail at something, do you prefer to move along rather than try again?

35. Would you say your work and free time are equally organized?

36. Would you feel vulnerable and somewhat helpless if you were fired from your job?

37. Are you dissatisfied with your job because you have not been promoted as often as you want or are not earning as much as you want?

38. Has anyone ever accused you of dishonesty in a work relationship?

39. Would you say you had a broad liberal arts education (with or without a degree)?

40. Do people often come to you to ask your help and advice on a wide variety of problems?

41. Do you tend to focus more on what is negative than positive in your life?

42. Do you feel you want many of the same things your peers at work want?

43. Is it important to you to keep up with current fashion?

44. When appliances break down, do you usually replace them rather than having them repaired?

45. Do you find yourself attracted only to a select group of people and feel that you have little to learn from the majority?

46. Are you attracted to the dark side of things?

47. If you had the time, would you prefer to do your own domestic chores?

48. Do you doubt your problem-solving skills when the unexpected occurs?

49. When seemingly insurmountable problems develop, do you "minimize your losses" by walking away rather than staying with them until they are resolved?

50. Do you often complain that you are exhausted?

If you scored *fewer than 10 wrong answers* (don't count "not sure" answers), read on and see if you recognize yourself in the following portrait drawn from successful ex-FTers.

Answers: 1(yes)   2(yes)   3(yes)   4(no)   5(yes)   6(yes)   7(no) 8(yes)   9(no)   10(yes) 11(yes) 12(yes) 13(yes) 14(no)   15(no)   16(yes) 17(yes) 18(no)   19(no)   20(no)   21(no)   22(yes) 23(yes) 24(no)   25(yes) 26(yes) 27(no)   28(no)   29(yes) 30(yes) 31(yes) 32(yes) 33(yes) 34(no) 35(yes) 36(no)   37(no)   38(no)   39(yes) 40(yes) 41(no)   42(no)   43(no) 44(no)   45(no)   46(no)   47(yes) 48(no)   49(no)   50(no)

The following traits are common among successful ex-FTers. They have been gleaned from observations of those who successfully left the fast track and from a variety of other sources, including Paul Hawken's book *Growing a Business*; Madeleine and Robert Swain's *Out the Organization*; and Marsha Sinetar's *Do What You Love, The Money Will Follow*. You may see a pattern that is or is not you. Successful ex-FTers, as a rule, had *all* of these characteristics and credit them for their success.

1. You are fiercely independent and self-sufficient.

2. You have boundless energy and vitality.

3. You are a conserver, not a consumer.

4. You have a keen sense of humor.

5. You don't rely on others' approval.

6. You try again if you fail.

7. You are trustworthy.

8. You take risks with a strong conviction.

9. You are eager for change and prepared for the unexpected.

10. You are willing to sacrifice.

11. You tend to question the status quo.

12. You accept criticism easily.

13. You take the initiative and make decisions.

14. You are an optimist.

15. You are tenacious, willing to persevere.

16. You spend time doing the things you enjoy most.

17. You are highly organized.

18. You are patient, a good listener, and willing to learn from others.

19. You are a problem solver and a hard worker.

20. You are happy with who you are and what you have.

21. You are creative and imaginative.

22. You take heed of your inner values.

Let's take each point in turn:

1. *You are fiercely independent and self-sufficient.*
These traits are the result of having extreme confidence in both your work and your life. You are a self-starter and you are able to work in any type of environment, be it an office, a back room, or the garage. You are ready and willing to go it alone. You can take control of your life and provide for yourself and your family.

2. *You have boundless energy and vitality.*
Psychiatrists say that most fatigue comes out of negative emotional and mental attitudes. J. A. Hadfield, a British psychiatrist, wrote in his book *The Psychology of Modern Problems* that the "greater part of the fatigue from which we suffer is of mental origin; in fact, exhaustion of purely physical origin is rare." Emotional and mental attitudes that cause fatigue include boredom, resentment, hostility, low self-esteem, anxiety, futility, jealousy, and tension. People who love their work and who choose exactly how they want to live their lives rarely suffer fatigue associated with these negative attitudes.

3. *You are a conserver, not a consumer.*
It doesn't embarrass you to be thrifty, to barter, to buy second-hand goods, to wait for the end-of-the-year sale. You save rather

than spend. You buy what you need and will use, not what you simply want and may waste. Your self-esteem does not depend on appearing prosperous.

Frame your mind to mirth and merriment,
Which bars a thousand harms and lengthens life.

Servant, in Shakespeare's
The Taming of the Shrew

4. *You have a keen sense of humor.* You find the ridiculous in the worst of circumstances. Your sense of humor protects you from the disappointments and setbacks that can cause others to feel angry, resentful, and helpless. It is a declaration of your superiority over adversity.

5. *You don't rely on others' approval.*
You do not need a job title or the trappings of an organization to give you self-worth. You believe in yourself. If any of the successful ex-FTers had worried about what their neighbors, associates, friends, or bosses thought of their "getting out," they never would have done it. Breaking away from the pack and striking out on one's own does not always win the approval of those who can't come along. Marsha Sinetar writes in *Do What You Love, The Money Will Follow*:

The one who loves his work, the actualizing person, has progressed as a personality despite his fears or angers. He is one who "has light" in himself. . . . He is an attractive, wholesome, luminous personality who does not require approval, status symbols and rewards from others. He does not—unlike the workaholic—crave outward shows of respect and rank (e.g., titles, large offices, special parking spaces, top floor suites) in order to continue manifesting, striving, "playing," and enjoying what he does. He strives, he does the work because he loves it, because in doing it he develops himself more completely, draws upon hidden inner reserves and abilities and creates from the depths of his being and imagination.

6. *You try again if you fail.*
Survival comes before success. Every ex-FTer has a story illustrating how he or she forged success from the knowledge and experience of a failure. Failure is a tool to use, not something to be frightened of. "Disappointment is natural, but paralyzing depression is not," wrote the Swains in *Out the Organization*.

Courage, resiliency, and determination characterize the successful ex-FTer. Dean Simonton, professor of psychology at the University of California at Davis and author of *Genius, Creativity and Leadership*, points out, "Great geniuses make tons of mistakes. They generate lots of ideas, and they accept being wrong. They have a kind of internal fortress that allows them to fail and just keep going. Look at Edison. He held over 1,000 patents, but most of them are not only forgotten, they weren't worth much to begin with."

7. *You are trustworthy.*
   Your handshake is as good as a contract. It is the reason you have had, and will have, repeat business dealings and long-term relationships with others.

8. *You take risks with a strong conviction.*
   Risk becomes opportunity when the risk-taker believes in what he is doing. You take your foot off first base because you just *know* you can make it to second. Many successful ex-FTers were willing to invest their savings to start out anew. They know full well that enterprise consists of confident action in the face of uncertainty.

9. *You are eager for change and prepared for the unexpected.*
   Adversity, not complacency, nurtures strength and courage. You keep your daily life in order and can cope with the disorder and chaos that comes with unforeseen setbacks and misfortune. Life's ups and downs are met with equanimity.

10. *You are willing to sacrifice.*
    When others are living for the moment, spending money on vacations, a new car, going out to dinner, buying material goods impulsively, you do without. You handle your time, energy, and money with extreme care. You do this wholeheartedly knowing it is part of your overall plan to live the good life.

    > Where there is an open mind, there will always be a frontier.
    >
    > CHARLES KETTERING
    > quoted in *Profile of America*

11. *You tend to question the status quo.*
    Many ex-FTers display a high level of self-awareness and personal freedom. They are able to break comfortable ties to the past

and move away from habitual behavior and a lifestyle considered secure and "successful" by society's pecuniary standards. What others find comforting, you find stagnating.

12. *You accept criticism easily.*
When you are able to accept criticism, you can learn from and welcome the constructive kind and ignore the destructive kind. You never interrupt when someone offers advice or a different idea.

13. *You take the initiative and make decisions.*
You make things happen. You direct your own destiny by taking control of your work, your time, and your life.

14. *You are an optimist.*
Cheerfulness and positive thinking are two of your strongest traits. You have a curiosity about the world around you, a healthy imagination, and an unselfish appreciation for people and things.

> It is the characteristic excellence of the strong man that he can bring momentous issues to the fore and make a decision about them. The weak are always forced to decide between alternatives they have not chosen themselves.
>
> Dietrich Bonhoeffer
> "Miscellaneous Thoughts" in
> *Letters and Papers from Prison*

> Life is a dynamic process. It welcomes anyone who takes up the invitation to be an active part of it. What we call the secret of happiness is no more a secret than our willingness to choose life.
>
> Leo Buscaglia
> *Bus 9 to Paradise*

15. *You are tenacious, willing to persevere.*
Some might call it stubbornness. You are determined to do things your way. When you make a commitment, you stick with it.

16. *You spend time doing the things you enjoy most.*
You have an unembarrassed appreciation for leisure, whether you spend your leisure time playing ping-pong with the kids, raising blue-ribbon orchids, swinging in the hammock, or learning to play the piano.

17. *You are highly organized.*
You have a game plan and a sense of order that enable you to take full advantage when opportunity arises. Being organized enables you to deal swiftly with the demands, problems, and endless details that go with making a change in environment and career.

18. *You are patient, a good listener, and willing to learn from others.*
You enjoy people. You believe that every person you meet may have something to teach you.

19. *You are a problem solver and a hard worker.*
You have the uncanny ability to solve problems in an unconventional way, and you look for simple answers that cost less. You work hard at tasks and find enjoyment in doing so.

20. *You are happy with who you are and what you have.*
You have a strong sense of self-esteem and an acceptance of, and gratitude for, what you have in life.

21. *You are creative and imaginative.*
Psycholinguist Vera John-Steiner, a creativity researcher, said in an article called "Creative Spin" in *Psychology Today* (March, 1989) that creative thought is a " 'search for meaning,' a way to connect our inner sense of being with some aspect of the world that preoccupies us." She believes that only by linking these two aspects of reality—the inner and the outer—can we gain "some sense of being in control of life." Successful ex-FTers tap into their creative and imaginative capabilities to create opportunity for themselves and to combat obstacles in their paths.

> Even when walking in a party of no more than three I can always be certain of learning from those I am with. There will be good qualities that I can select for imitation and bad ones that will teach me what requires correction in myself.
>
> CONFUCIUS

22. *You take heed of your inner values.*
This comes from having a personal vision of happiness and practicing one's own code of ethics. Marsha Sinetar writes that self-actualized people are "creative, independent, and self-sufficient" and that they have "as their primary focus personal goals, inner values, and the creation of distinct lifestyles." They have "the ability to perceive their own delights and values, have rediscovered their own selves, and now wish to merge that self with vocational and life activities."

Do you fit the profile? Only you can answer that question, and it requires complete honesty. Are you a risk-taker? Will you persevere through failures? Do you want this more than anything else? Are you completely confident that you can pull it off? Are you comfortable about your reasons for wanting to get off the fast track? Do you believe you have what it takes?

Belief in oneself comes out of the assumption that you have the ideas, the knowledge, the experience, and the skills to be what you want to be.

Another way of looking at this "belief in oneself" is to understand it as a source of energy within each of us that is there when we most need it. Tarthang Tulku, a lama from Eastern Tibet, speaks of this energy in terms of "skillful means" in his book *Skillful Means*: "By using skillful means to enrich our lives and bring our creative potential into everything we do, we can penetrate to the heart of our true nature. We then gain an understanding of the basic purpose of life, and appreciate the joy of making good use of our precious time and energy."

> Our belief at the beginning of a doubtful undertaking is the one thing that ensures the successful outcome of the venture.
>
> WILLIAM JAMES
> *The Varieties of Religious Experience*

Believing you can do it is a combination of inner resourcefulness and external preparation. Confidence is born from having a well-thought-out plan of action with no missing elements. There is a difference between blind faith and faith that is the result of having done your homework. A fair percentage of successful ex-FTers spoke of their blind faith and their "strokes of luck." In truth, these individuals have paved the way for "luck" to enter their lives. Richard Bolles, in his book *What Color Is Your Parachute?*, suggests a few ways to open the door to this luck:

1. Luck favors the prepared mind.

2. Luck favors the person who is working the hardest . . . doing their research, making contacts.

3. Luck favors the person who has told the most people clearly and precisely what he or she is looking for.

4. Luck favors the person who has alternatives up his or her sleeve.

5. Luck favors the person who WANTS WITH ALL THEIR HEART . . .

6. Luck favors the person who is going after their dream—the thing they really want to do the most in this world.

7. Luck favors the person who is trying hard to be "a special kind of person" in this world, treating others with grace and dignity and courtesy and kindness.

ARE YOU RUNNING *FROM,* OR SEARCHING *FOR*?

It is important to distinguish between the urge to run *away from problems* and the urge to *search for something better.* If what is making you unhappy is an external complaint or difficulty, you may run the risk of relocating and discovering that those external problems you hoped to escape have simply been replaced by different problems. The external complaints are not always reason enough to initiate a drastic change in career and environment. External reasons for wanting out can include: problems at the office, neglect of family and friends, stiff mortgages, consumer debt, traffic, pollution, and the stress of city living.

> Our life is what our thoughts make it.
>
> MARCUS AURELIUS

For example, consider the individual eager to escape the noise and pollution of the city. She relocates to a rural environment only to discover that summer mosquitoes and humidity, and winter ice and subzero temperatures, are worse than what she left behind. Another example is the fast-tracker who hates the competitive atmosphere at his company. He relocates to a smaller city and discovers that office politics are even more magnified in a closer-knit community.

For every negative reason to leave, you may find a negative trade-off waiting in the wings: hostile neighbors, boredom, severe weather conditions, floods, tornadoes, drought, mosquitoes, ticks, deerflies, limited entertainment, few restaurants, depressed local economies, religious fanatics, high energy costs, polarized politics, limited services, poor medical facilities, no private schools, polluted lákes, toxic dumps, poor educational facilities—you name it, wherever you go, there will be drawbacks to the area.

Marion Kaire, a former Los Angeles restaurateur who traded her $140,000 home in Sylmar (CA) for a $50,000 home in the pine forests of the central Oregon coast, says that the air is "sparkling clean" but it's also so cold and rainy there that "a lot of people come up here, stay for two years and then go someplace else." (*Los Angeles Times,* March 3, 1989)

Jill Hearing says she lived in Washington six months before her neighbors would talk to her. "I didn't know when I first moved up here that Californians were the hated enemy. . . . In California, we always had more of an open mind. People accepted you as long as you were honorable or hard-working. Here [the attitude is], "If my aunt doesn't know you and want to give you a good recommendation, we don't want to know you." . . . Despite 20 years' experience as a pipe fitter and a good work record, it took Hearing's husband almost a year to find work in Seattle. And when he did, it was a two-hour commute by bus and ferryboat. . . . Hearing pays 79 cents a pound for bananas, twice what she did in Garden Grove. And to heat her house with electricity cost $50 a week. . . . If she and her husband had it to do over, Hearing says, "I would not, knowing what I know now, come up here." (Los Angeles Times, March 3, 1989)

It is important that your reasons for making the move are reasons that can't be affected by the trade-offs. If your motivations for wanting out are positive, motivations that come from within, you won't find the trade-offs to be insurmountable setbacks.

We greatly enjoyed our city life, and that may be the key to the even greater enjoyment we experience beyond the sidewalks. People tend to remain the same wherever they are. Had we been miserable in the city, we doubtless would be miserable where we presently are. . . . Coming here from the busy, bustling city was like stepping into a different world. There are many long hours of hard physical work, obstacles to overcome and new things to be learned daily, but we enjoy every bit of it. (Countryside, August, 1982)

MARY BROWN
Riverside, CA

Getting out for the wrong reason can sabotage one's chances of making a successful transition to a simpler way of life. Vic Sussman, a journalist, returned to the city to live the simple life after discovering that for him, living in the country was a lot more complicated.

I lived in Vermont for five years and I realize now that I was angry most of the time. There was always this oppressive sense of being behind—behind in the garden, behind with getting in the wood supply. And for what? Weeding carrots just wasn't enough for me. I thrive on contact with people, but you don't meet that many people in the woods. And the natives weren't exactly scintillating company. . . . When I lived in the country, I used to preach about living the simple life, with *Walden* as my text. I took *Walden* at face value—I read it as an exhortation to "live deliberately in the woods." What I sometimes forgot was that Henry Thoreau's cabin was only a mile from his mother's house and that he often went home for dinner. . . . I think I'm living the simple life now, in the city. I wake up in the morning and the furnace is running, the pipes aren't freezing. That's simplicity. I love it. The other day I was downtown eating fast Indian food, my girlfriend was eating fast Chinese food and I was in heaven. . . . I'm still gardening— but now I'm cultivating myself instead of the earth. (*Harrowsmith*, March, 1987)

If external complaints are your sole motivation for wanting out, you would be wise to reassess your situation and your needs, looking to solutions in your everyday life before packing up and heading elsewhere. Leonard Schlesinger, a professor at the Harvard Business School, says that a growing number of executives and managers are stepping onto the "sanity track." Although they are remaining at their jobs, they are turning down promotions, cutting back on business travel, and working fewer hours in order to devote more time to their families, their friends, and themselves. Such alternatives to getting out completely are discussed in chapter 7.

TAKING TIME OUT TO DECIDE

If you are confused and at a loss about what you should do— whether you should attempt to get off the fast track or whether you should instead stay where you are and make a few changes—take Joseph Campbell's advice and *take time out.* Find quiet time every day to spend by yourself and think things over. Campbell describes the process this way: "You must have a room, or a certain hour or so a day, where you don't know what was in the newspapers that morning, you don't know who your friends are, you don't know what you owe anybody, you don't know what anybody owes to you. This is a place where you can simply experience and bring forth what you are and what you

> This is your life, and nobody is going to teach you—no book, no guru. You have to learn from yourself, not from books. It is an endless thing, it is a fascinating thing, and when you learn about yourself from yourself, out of that learning wisdom comes. Then you can live a most extraordinary, happy, beautiful life.
>
> J. KRISHNAMURTI

might be. This is the place of creative incubation. At first you may find that nothing happens there. But if you have a sacred place and use it, something will eventually happen."

By reaching for a more intimate knowledge of your inner self, you will learn what makes you different from everyone else: your talents, your skills, your unique insights and perceptions of the people and the world around you. This will help give your life direction and purpose, and it will help you to develop your personal vision of happiness. Out of these quiet moments will come the positive reasons for wanting a change in your life. You may discover that the life you are leading now *can* make you happy, and that your motivations for wanting to escape have been spurred by superficial problems or shortcomings that can be dealt with more pragmatically.

Whatever the case, you need to take time out and reclaim your spirit. Sooner or later, you will be spurred to action, whatever that may be. Chapter 3 will help you to define the good life for yourself. It offers guidance in recognizing priorities, focusing objectives, and devising a game plan for achieving what is now missing in your life.

SUGGESTED READING

BARITZ, LOREN. *The Good Life*. New York: Harper & Row, 1982.

BERRY, WENDELL. *The Unsettling of America: Culture and Agriculture*. San Francisco: Sierra Club Books, 1977.

BLOOM, ALLAN. *The Closing of the American Mind*. New York: Simon and Schuster, 1987.

CAMPBELL, JOSEPH. *The Power of Myth*. New York: Doubleday, 1988.

FIELDS, RICK, et al. *Chop Wood, Carry Water*. Los Angeles: Jeremy Tarcher, 1984.

HILL, NAPOLEON. *Think and Grow Rich*. New York: Fawcett Crest, 1960.

LASCH, CHRISTOPHER. *The Culture of Narcissism: American Life in an Age of Diminishing Expectations*. New York: Norton, 1978.

MAY, ROLLO. *Man's Search for Himself*. New York: Dell Publishing, 1965.

REICH, CHARLES. *The Greening of America*. New York: Random House, 1970.

SHAMES, LAWRENCE. *The Hunger for More*. New York: Times Books, 1989.

SHI, DAVID E. *In Search of the Simple Life*. Salt Lake City: Peregrine Smith, 1986.

STORR, ANTHONY. *Solitude*. New York: Ballantine Books, 1988.

THOREAU, HENRY DAVID. *On the Duty of Civil Disobedience*. New York: Harper & Row, 1965.

3

To laugh often and much;
To win the respect of intelligent people
    and the affection of children;
To earn the appreciation of honest critics
    and endure the betrayal of false friends:
To appreciate beauty;
To find the best in others;
To leave the world a bit better, whether by
    a healthy child, a garden patch
    or a redeemed social condition;
To know even one life has breathed
    easier because you have lived;
This is to have succeeded.

RALPH WALDO EMERSON

In Search of the Good Life

WHOLESALE STOCKBROKER TURNED COWBOY

The dirt road leading to Redington Land & Cattle Co. is running a foot deep in fast-moving water at three different places. The rain may be the reason a couple of wranglers heading into the brush on horseback respond with silence and surly expressions when asked where to park a car.

The odor of wet manure and wet desert hangs in the air around the pipe corrals and tack sheds leading to what appears to be an antiquated depot for stagecoach arrivals. Inside a small, dark room fragrant with the smell of leather and fresh coffee sits Don Steinman, surrounded by cavalry guns, saddles, books, stagecoach memorabilia, and enough of his favorite things to limit any sudden movements. A multiple-line phone at his elbow interrupts him repeatedly.

"What you are speaks so loudly I cannot hear you." That's Emerson and that was me. I'd fallen into the solid gold trap. I had the English tudor estate featured in *HG* on Philadelphia's Mainline.

45

My wife, I remember, was throwing a $25,000 party and I was looking at my life asking myself where in hell was I?

It hit me in Penn Station at rush hour. I looked down at my shirtcuffs soaked with sweat and I said, "I quit." That was it. I turned everything over to my ex-wife and left with my horse, my saddle, and my gun. There are some things not even the IRS can take away from you.

For 22 years I was syndicating tax shelters for the big boys in real estate, oil, horses, ranches—you name it. After you make so many million dollars, cash becomes just one more commodity. For me the reward was the deal, the thrill of cutting the deal. I still get calls asking me to do a little consultation and I stay away from it—I'm liable to make money!

I don't own this outfit. The land is leased and 60% of the herd is owned by somebody else. A Wall Street hotshot will come here and put $1,000 down on a horse so he can say that's his horse whenever he's here. We feed the horse, keep it fit, and get the use of it when the owner's not around. Not a bad deal. I have the premier operation—more horses, and the best wranglers. I have enough talent here to run IBM. Some of our people are PhD's and volunteer to work here.

When I dropped out, I did some consulting work on the side, but basically I just rode my horse for two years and was nearly broke. I remember when my truck broke down out on the highway and I didn't have money to fix it and I didn't have anyone to call who could help me. When that happened I felt a deep panic and it was a telling moment, all right—the kind that will make or break you.

My girlfriend Barb and I may be wondering where the truck payment for this month is going to come from, but I know none of us is going to starve to death. We do a lot of bartering around here. I get my trucks repaired by a fella keeps his mules here. One wrangler needed cash bad so I loaned him $200 against his saddle. Someday he'll be back and his saddle will be waiting for him.

Barb puts up with a lot. She was a former account executive, had a beautiful townhouse, and here she has given it all up to live like this—but she's happy.

You have to have the wisdom to recognize opportunity when it comes your way. If you keep a watchful eye, jump at opportunities, be careful you don't stick it to anybody, help out those you can, well then, it's a wonderful life. Live well and live right. Be honest and never compromise your ethics. I was an Eagle Scout, and I think it's the basis for what I value.

Before I came out here, I had a great horse, Night Patrol, who had belonged to the Philadelphia Police Department. I remember one day when I was riding and Night Patrol went off the road toward a patch of daisies and stood there sniffing them. It was a message to me right then and there that I'd better stop and smell the flowers, too, or it was going to be too late. The most precious gift is today, and you have to take care of it.

I feel more secure in my life today than I ever did before. To make life a success, you need vitality and a challenge. Getting what you really want takes faith, confidence, and a lot of self-respect. People today lose sight of who they really are.

This operation contributes to over 30 charities. That kind of work is not income-producing and yet good things come to us every time we put ourselves out for somebody. One year for the Grant-A-Wish project we got a bunch of kids out of their wheel-chairs, got them onto the hay wagon, and took them bouncing into the mountains. The look on those kids' faces!

I've stayed at the Marquis and the Biltmore, and I'd take a bedroll under the stars any day. My grandfather left Russia with nothing. I come from pioneering stock. Only a handful out there can drop out. Of the others, 80% would like to but don't have what it takes. "Make it happen," said Vince Lombardi. You have to have guts.

DON STEINMAN
Stable Manager
Tucson, Arizona

BOOKING AGENT AND ART DIRECTOR TURNED INNKEEPERS

Every morning at eight, Christian Andrade feeds his chickens and sees to it that his guests are also fed before he drives his pickup truck to the ferry dock on San Juan Island to pick up newspapers. He is the local distributor on this island off the northwest coast of Washington. After distributing the newspapers to a few key locations, he will return to Olympic Lights, the bed-and-breakfast inn he runs with his wife Lea, and together they will continue housekeeping chores and making phone calls before morning is half over.

We were the type of people who said we would never leave San Francisco. Lea was an art director for Wells Fargo Bank, and I was a meeting planner. We had considered Monterey or Carmel as places we might consider moving to in the future, but at that time we weren't really burned out. We just thought a change might be nice someday.

By chance, we had friends who were on San Juan Island on some house-swapping deal, and we decided to visit them. We fell in love with the island instantly. Lea said on the ferry over that she felt like she was coming home. You can call it nature or a spirit, but there was something about this place that felt good and very right. That was in May, and by November we had moved there permanently and were beginning our bed-and-breakfast business.

We knew we needed a business to survive, and we didn't want to work for anybody else. We came back three weeks after our initial visit and began looking for property, and we found this Victorian farmhouse. Our friends and family all said we were crazy. We had a beautiful Victorian home in San Francisco that we had designed and renovated, and we had a Japanese garden. Everything was finally perfect after all of our hard work, and here we were ready to sell the house, quit our successful careers, and line up the rental trucks!

It has been very easy fitting into this community. Everyone is very friendly and welcoming. We're more involved in the community here and we've done some nonprofit charitable things, including an auction and a square dance for wildlife rehabilitation.

We have also become closer to the land and to wildlife. We see the stars at night, and the sunrise in the morning. We are a lot more appreciative of the planet. We are very active in environmental issues and animal rights. And the only stress I feel these days is when we drive into the city.

The best advice I can offer anyone is to clarify what it is you want. Then, you have to realize fully that there will be a lot of hurdles to getting there. But you can overcome them, whether friends or family or what you read about is against you. We all have the power within ourselves to acquire what we want. Some people just aren't aware of it.

CHRISTIAN AND LEA ANDRADE
Innkeepers
San Juan Island, Washington

WHAT IS "THE GOOD LIFE"?

The American concept of the good life is rooted in the writings of such American idealists as John Winthrop, William Penn, Thomas Jefferson, Ralph Waldo Emerson, Henry David Thoreau, John Burroughs, Wendell Berry, and dozens of others. Many of them have drawn upon the writings of Aristotle, Epictetus, Marcus Aurelius, and other classical philosophers who emphasized the value of honest work, life in the country, personal autonomy, social responsibility, spiritual ideals, and virtuous activity. In his book *In Search of the Simple Life*, David Shi sums up this traditional perspective of the good life:

> A concern for family nurture and community cohesion; a hostility toward luxury; . . . a belief that the primary reward of work should be well-being rather than money; a desire for maximum personal self-reliance and creative leisure; a nostalgia for the supposed simplicities of the past; . . . a taste for the plain and functional, especially in the home environment; a reverence for nature and a preference for country-living; and a sense of both religious and ecological responsibility for the proper use of the world's resources. What unifies this cluster of attitudes is the conscious desire to purge life of some of its complexities and superfluities in order to pursue "higher" values—faith, family, civic duty, artistic creativity, and social service.

In the eyes of American idealists, the good life was an attempt to elevate one's aspirations beyond the materialistic. It was an attempt at living a life of simplicity that allowed the individual time to wonder at and appreciate the simple joys in life. To live the good life was to be able to control one's life and one's destiny, and not be at the mercy of the marketplace. It meant plain living and high intent devoted to family, civic, and spiritual ideals. It had much to do with hard work, self-discipline, commitment, perseverance in the face of adversity, and at the same time an unembarrassed appreciation for leisure and solitude—time for personal enlightenment and time to relish one's blessings.

Today's ex-FTers find themselves in search of many of the things that have historically been associated with the good life. The key ingredients (not in order of importance) that make up that historical vision are these:

Appreciating the Simple Things in Life

Doing What You Long to Do

Living Plainly

Counting Your Blessings

High Thinking

Nurturing Relationships with Family and Friends

Virtuous Activity, Social Responsibility

In the next pages, we'll explore each of these concepts in turn.

Appreciating the Simple Things in Life

In an essay entitled "What Life Means to Me," published in *Cosmopolitan* in 1906, naturalist John Burroughs wrote about what it means to live the good life:

> I am bound to praise the simple life, because I have lived it and found it good. When I depart from it, evil results follow. I love a small house, plain clothes, simple living. Many persons know the luxury of a skin bath—a plunge in the pool or the wave—unhampered by clothing. That is the simple life—direct and immediate contact with things, life with the false wrappings torn away—the fine house, the fine equipage, the expensive habits, all cut off. How free one feels, how good the elements taste, how close one gets to them, how they fit one's body and one's soul! . . . To be in direct and personal contact with the sources of your material life; to want no extras, no shields; to find the universal elements enough; to find the air and the water exhilarating; to be refreshed by a morning walk, or an evening saunter; to find a quest of wild berries more satisfying than a gift of tropic fruit; to be thrilled by the stars at night; to be elated over a bird's nest, or over a wild flower in spring—these are some of the rewards of the simple life.

The loss of "direct and immediate contact with things" is a common complaint among today's victims of the rat race. Those who have successfully escaped the fast track tell of the newfound rewards. They talk of the simple things in life that they now have time for: walking to work, cooking with home-grown vegetables and fruit, hiking in the country, taking piano lessons, eating ice cream in the park, going to a Sunday matinee, reading more books, making Halloween costumes, watching thunderstorms, tying flies, keeping a journal, attending the local potluck supper, acting in the community play, savoring the moonlight, sleeping out under the stars . . .

> We seldom think of what we have but always of what we lack.
>
> Schopenhauer

On the very traditional end of the scale for those appreciating the simple life are the Dixons and the Dwinells.

With the greenhouse we built, we have started a small herb and wildflower business to supplement our lodging business. We have blended what we think are the best of traditional and modern ways to give our lives the right balance of responsibility and relaxation, hard work and fun. We are educating our daughters at home, because there are no schools where we live. Carl goes out and starts the diesel generator that brings power to the house; I turn on our computer, and our four-year-old learns to use a keyboard with a simple preschool program. She also learns how to stay clear of a moose on a trail while skiing and the signs to watch out for on an iced-over river that might be getting ready for spring breakup. We hope our daughters will know the best that life has to offer. (*Harrowsmith*, March, 1988)

KIRSTEN AND CARL DIXON
Fishing Lodge Owners
Lake Creek, Alaska

I sit here in the peacefulness of winter, looking out the window from the top loft. The blue jays and the red squirrel share the birdfeeder; a downy woodpecker is at the suet. I see my husband, Sky, and our draft horse, Lil, arrive with another log to add to the growing pile in the yard. A portable sawmill will come in the spring to saw those logs into lumber for the "big house" that we plan to build this year. . . . I see our daughter, Dana, asleep in her crib and the cats cuddled together on the bed. I am content. I am here. My dream has come true . . . simple living, making do with what you have and doing for yourself as much as possible. Providing our own power, heat, food, lumber and skills is deeply satisfying. I feel safe; I feel secure; I feel proud. . . . As for cash flow, we make do. My husband is training to be a mediator. My nursing degree comes in handy as I suspected; part-time and on-call work is always available. We have a small home business making fresh salsa, which is sold in health food stores and co-ops around the state. When the house is done, we will build a sugarhouse and start maple sugaring again. . . . Barter also works well around here. (*Harrowsmith*, March, 1988)

JANE AND SKY DWINELL
Entrepreneurs
Irasburg, Vermont

Doing What You Long to Do

Many ex-FTers have come to understand that how you spend your working day is how you spend your life. To separate life from work is to sacrifice one or the other. They felt the sting of that sacrifice and found it intolerable, for the quality of one's work ultimately equals the quality of one's life. This knowledge of what Buddhists call "right livelihood," coupled with a strong sense of purpose and direction in life, is an essential aspect of knowing who you are and what you want. *Chop Wood, Carry Water* quotes Theodore Roszak's description of the Buddhist concept of right livelihood:

> The Buddha, in his wisdom, made "right livelihood". . . one of the steps to enlightenment. If we do not pitch our discussion that high, we have failed to give work its true dimension, and we will settle for far too little—perhaps for no more than a living wage. Responsible work is an embodiment of love, and love is the only discipline that will serve in shaping the personality, the only discipline that makes the mind whole and constant for a lifetime of effort. There hovers about a true vocation that paradox of all significant self-knowledge—our capacity to find ourselves by losing ourselves. We lose ourselves in our love of the task before us, and in that moment we learn an identity that lives both within and beyond us.

An essential feature of the good life is working at an occupation that you have a talent for instead of at a job that you do mainly to earn a lot of money. Khalil Gibran's statement that "work is love made visible" is an ancient concept that has been largely forgotten in modern times. Only recently has it captured our imaginations as we discover that success is not defined by material wealth but by personal achievement and accomplishments of lasting value.

> "You don't have to be trained to instinctively feel when something is right, made with love and care. . . . There's an aura about such a thing which calls attention to itself." The attention the press [Yolla Bolly Press] has drawn comes from farflung reaches of the country, and beyond. In their remote rural setting, the Robertsons receive more requests for apprenticeships than they can accept, and their customers stretch across the globe. . . . "We both know what we like to do, and we just keep doing it, day after day, with discipline and a focused concentration of energy. There are no

distractions here, nobody luring you to lunch or a movie," says Carolyn Robertson. What she and her husband have found, she says, is that, as people who deeply love the work they do, they "are rewarded so many times over, simply by being able to do it. You can never learn it all, and it keeps feeding you and confirming you, giving you an ever-renewable lease on creativity." (*Horizon*, November, 1988)

JAMES AND CAROLYN ROBERTSON
Publishers
Covelo, California

Less and less is being written about today's money-makers as people become more intrigued with those "eccentrics" who are doing what they always wanted to do without regard to how much money they make. It is not the professional earning six figures we are in awe of, but the craftsman who has retrieved the lost art of blacksmithing; the farmer who raises pesticide-free produce; the factory worker who buys out management, takes a pay cut, and works to produce better quality goods; the teacher who devotes extra time to students.

What do such people have in common? All of them love their work and take great pride in it. They work at jobs that come naturally to them. Using their unique talents and special skills, they work hard, putting in what many of them like to call "an honest day's work," and thereby attaining an unequaled feeling of acomplishment and satisfaction.

> The reward of a thing well done is to have done it.
>
> EMERSON

The freedom to choose one's work is a freedom lost to many of today's fast-trackers, who not only are dependent on their employers but also have a great fear of living without a high income. William James wrote about the corruption that goes hand in hand with the obsession to earn a lot of money. That obsession can lead fast-trackers to become slaves to their possessions, and no longer free to change their lives at a whim. In *The Varieties of Religious Experience*, William James wrote:

We despise any one who elects to be poor in order to simplify and save his inner life. If he does not join the general scramble and pant with the money-making street, we deem him spiritless and lacking in ambition. We have lost the power even of imagining what the ancient idealization of poverty could have meant: the liberation from material attachments, the unbribed soul, the manlier indifference, the paying our way by what we are or do and not by what we have, the right to fling away our life at any moment irresponsibly. . . . The desire to gain wealth and the fear to lose it are our chief breeders of cowardice and propagators of corruption.

In *The Good Life*, Loren Baritz writes that an end result of today's price to succeed is indeed costly: "life as work, the happiness produced by objects, the envy of strangers, and the freedom to float above the struggles of others, in warmth and comfort, alone."

Successful ex-FTers talk about working at jobs that allow them to express their creativity, their joy, and their fullness as human beings. It is not unlike the Buddhist concept of right livelihood, which sees work as a way to deepen and enrich one's life by using every aspect of work to learn and grow. The desire for right livelihood comes from within, from a deeper understanding of who we are and the recognition of our special talents. Such work is more personally satisfying and is the type of work that society benefits from. In their book *Living the Good Life*, Helen and Scott Nearing wrote about the importance of enjoying one's work.

> Blessed is he who expects little, but works as if he expected much. . . . For anything worth having one must pay the price, and the price is always work, patience, love, self-sacrifice—no paper currency, no promises to pay, but the gold of real service.
>
> JOHN BURROUGHS

Each day was divided into two main blocks of time—four morning hours and four afternoon hours. . . . Then by agreement we decided which of these blocks of time should be devoted to bread labor and which to personally determined activities. . . . . One might read, write, sit in the sun, walk in the woods, play music, go to town. We earned our four hours of leisure by our four hours of labor. . . . We took our time, every day, every month, every year. We had our work, did it and enjoyed it. We had our leisure, used it and enjoyed that. . . . We have never worked harder and have never enjoyed work more, because, with rare exceptions, the work was significant, self-directed, constructive and therefore interesting.

The search for right livelihood involves the identification of one's talents, interests, aptitudes, and skills. It requires that you have your priorities in order and know what is most valuable in your life.

The good life has its price. Jon says his income is half of what it was. The Goodsons can't remember the last movie they went to. And learning the restaurant business overnight was a hit-and-miss proposition filled with seven-day workweeks. "You've got to want to do it more than anything else in the world," Meg says. "And then it works." (*USA Weekend*, September 14, 1990)

> JON AND MEG GOODSON
> *Nutritionists, Restaurateurs*
> *Kelly's Island, Ohio*

People working at their right livelihoods trust themselves. They listen to their inner voices, where they find strength and confidence. In *Skillful Means*, Tibetan Buddhist Tarthang Tulku wrote:

Caring about our work, liking it, even loving it, seems strange when we see work only as a way to make a living. But when we see work as the way to deepen and enrich all of our experience, each one of us can find this caring within our hearts, and awaken it in those around us, using every aspect of work to learn and grow. . . . Caring for our work, being really involved in it, is the secret of doing things well and of deriving satisfaction from whatever we do. When we care, an attitude of relaxed alertness nurtures and supports us. Our work becomes light and enjoyable, a source of deeper knowledge and appreciation.

Living Plainly

True security comes not from owning more possessions but from needing fewer of them. To live plainly is to distinguish between the necessary and the superfluous, between what you desire and what is in your best interest.

Although plain living involves practicing a measure of restraint, it offers relief from debt as well as security and freedom. Living plainly is not synonymous with the ascetic life or doing without; instead, it means living within one's

> Economy is a distributive virtue, and consists not in saving but in selection.
>
> EDMUND BURKE
> *Letter to a Noble Lord*

means. Successful ex-FTers do without extravagance and live secure, comfortable lives.

There are times when winter begins to drag and we feel a little envy for folks who can book the first available flight for Nassau and to hell with waiting for the charter deal. . . . But almost always the old habits prevail, and we keep our spending to careful limits. It's times like that when we need a pressure valve. Without some release, the constant discipline on money matters would begin to feel rigid and mean—more like a dreary trap than a means of freedom and independence. . . . That's when we throw another log on the grate, open a bottle of the best wild grape, and sit down to a juicy roast of loin or brace of squab. Candlelight, a little music and a crackling fire. By the end of the evening we're back to feeling grateful that the clunky old Ford can be patched again and there's at least another week of skiing left before the sap begins to run.

CHARLES LONG
How to Survive Without a Salary

Counting Your Blessings

In his book *The Examined Life*, Robert Nozick writes about two types of happiness. The first type is the result of feeling that your life is what you want it to be. This kind of happiness occurs as rare, wonderful moments when you find yourself not wanting anything but what you have. You feel a complete satisfaction. It might happen when you are with the one you love, when you are doing something you love to do, or when you are struck with the simple realization that your life is lacking nothing.

The second type of happiness is being satisfied with your life as a whole. This is usually the result of having a happy disposition and being able to focus on the positive side of life. In both cases, it requires the individual to acknowledge and appreciate what is positive and good in his or her life.

For many successful ex-FTers, their contentment is a natural outgrowth of the way they look at things. They speak with pleasure about the positive aspects of their lives including where they live, what they do for work, how happy their families are. They seem very grateful for what they have. When things go wrong, they have a natural tendency to look on the bright side.

> Happiness, whether consisting in pleasure or virtue, or both, is more often found with those who are highly cultivated in their mind and in their character, and have only a moderate share of external goods, than among those who possess external goods to a useless extent but are deficient in higher qualities.
>
> ARISTOTLE
> *Politics*

High Thinking

Part of living the good life is questioning and pondering the life one is living, working every day to make one's life more personally fulfilling and the world a better place. High thinking involves taking time out every day to renew our enthusiasm for life by learning something new. If our life becomes a process of learning and thinking, we deepen and broaden our own sense of freedom and independence.

> Instead of the hectic mad rush of busyness we intended a quiet pace, with time to wonder, ponder and observe. We hoped to replace worry, fear and hate with serenity, purpose and at-one-ness.
>
> HELEN AND SCOTT NEARING

When Timothy Dwight was president of Yale University he said: "The happiest person is the person who thinks the most interesting thoughts." Psychologist William McDougall had a similar idea when he made this statement: "The richer, the more highly developed, the more completely unified or integrated is the personality, the more capable it is of sustained happiness, in spite of intercurrent pains of all sorts."

Nurturing Relationships with Family and Friends

In her commencement speech at Wellesley College in 1990, Barbara Bush said, "At the end of your life, you will never regret not having passed one more test, winning one more verdict, or not closing one more deal. You will regret time not spent with a husband, a child, a friend, or a parent."

In *The Examined Life*, Robert Nozick writes, "There is no bond I know stronger than being a parent. Having children and raising them gives one's life substance. . . . The connection to a child certainly involves the deepest love. . . . Being a parent helps one become a better child, a more forgiving grown-up child of one's parents."

> The ornament of a house is the friends who frequent it.
>
> EMERSON
> *Society and Solitude*
>
> There is no hope of joy except in human relations.
>
> SAINT-EXUPÉRY
> *Wind, Sand, and Stars*

Families share a unique bond of common experience and a love that is strong and deep. They offer support in time of need, and give meaning to our existence. They are a key ingredient to our self-discovery.

Sociologist and Quaker Elise Boulding writes in *Friends Testimonies in the Home* of the importance of nurturing the home environment: "The truth is that the home is the training ground where people first learn to live with one another . . . how to love and work with other people, how to handle hate, anger and fear so that it does not destroy themselves or others . . . and experience the full depth of forgiveness in the give and take of family life."

When we nurture our relationships with family and friends, we nurture an atmosphere of affection, respect, and kindness. We feel a renewed self-esteem as we reach out to others. A sense of vitality and a feeling of harmony and well-being characterize the nurtured family.

Admiral Richard E. Byrd wrote his thoughts on happiness when he believed he was dying in the ice of the Ross Barrier: "I realized I had failed to see that the simple, homely, unpretentious things of life are the most important. When a man achieves a fair measure of harmony within himself and his family circle, he achieves peace. At the end only two things really matter to a man, regardless of who he is: the affection and understanding of his family."

Virtuous Activity, Social Responsibility

Aristotle's idea of happiness had much to do with ethics. Living the good life meant behaving in a virtuous manner, living a life of courage, wisdom, and self-control, and always striving to do the right thing. This is very different from the definition of happiness found in many self-help books, which in essence says that happiness means having a happy outlook and *feeling good*. Many ex-FTers discover a wonderful sense of community, working with others to promote the common good.

> It is not enough merely to possess virtue, as if it were an art; it should be practiced.
>
> MARCUS TULLIUS CICERO

Many successful ex-FTers participate in their communities by volunteering their time to charity, religious organizations, educational institutions, and civic and political groups. Nearly all feel that such volunteer work is an integral part of their new lives.

Environmental awareness is another facet of promoting the common good that is embraced by successful ex-FTers.

We know that we contribute to the human impact here. We make our living from guests coming to fish, but we promote a catch-and-release policy on fishing. We won't allow our guests to over-fish their legal limits, and we will not tolerate littering on our river. . . . We have also tried to limit our growth to what we feel is consistent with the environment. We accept only 12 guests.

KIRSTEN AND CARL DIXON
Fishing Lodge Owners
Lake Creek, Alaska

We've watched our generation spend a lot of their effort on things of very little value, like leveraged buyouts. For us, it is important to have a product that we really feel good about, that is good for the environment and for the people who are eating it. (*Countryside, Winter, 1990*)

ANTHONY AND SUSAN STEVENS
Organic Farmers
Martinsburg, West Virginia

In the arena of human life the honors and rewards fall to those who show their good qualities in action.

ARISTOTLE

The tone in which we speak to the world the world speaks to us. Give your best and you will get the best in return. Give in heaping measure and in heaping measure it shall be returned. We all get our due sooner or later, in one form or another. "Be not weary in well doing"; the reward will surely come, if not in worldly goods, then in inward satisfaction, grace of spirit, peace of mind.

JOHN BURROUGHS

CREATING A PERSONAL VISION OF THE GOOD LIFE

The following exercises will help you identify and clarify what you want most out of life, and then develop and focus objectives for achieving that vision.

Exercise 1: Imagining the Good Life
Exercise 2: Identifying the Positive and Negative Aspects of Your Life Today
Exercise 3: Focusing Your Objectives and Priorities
Exercise 4: Making the Big Decision and Setting Goals
Exercise 5: Making a Wish List

Buy yourself a journal or notebook of some type that you enjoy handling. You will use it to do these exercises, and you will also use it to compile the information you gather in your research throughout the rest of this book. (A three-ring binder with separate divisions or a special notebook in your computer will work well.) In your journal you will keep track of your priorities, your objectives, and your plan of action. Also, using the journal as "information central" and keeping all of your resource material in one place will help you stay efficient, organized, and clear-thinking.

Exercise 1: Imagining the Good Life
Begin this exercise when you can set aside quiet time for undisturbed thought. Write down every thought that comes to mind that means the good life to you. This is a personal exercise that should represent your own ideas of what will make you happy. Group each idea in one of these four categories:

> WORK
> FAMILY AND FRIENDS
> ENVIRONMENT
> YOURSELF

Under each heading, write down as many things as you can think of that you feel would give you "the good life." Try to create a mental picture of exactly what you want. The more clearly you can imagine it, the easier it will be to work with. If there are two of you, do the exercises together; if you do them separately, cross-reference and develop a vision that you both share. If you are a family, you will need everyone's input. The information you put together for these exercises will be especially useful in chapter 4.

For Example:

WORK

- I would continue earning my living as an accountant but only work part time.
- I would be my own boss and work out of my home.
- I'd work from 8 A.M. to noon during the week and maybe two hours in the evening.
- During the winter months, I'd also work part time as a ski instructor.

FAMILY and FRIENDS

- I would have afternoons free to spend with my family.

- Twice a week we would entertain and have friends over for dinner.

- We would go on outings on the weekends—hiking, river-rafting, cross-country skiing, and biking.

ENVIRONMENT

- We would live near a winter resort community in the mountains.

- We would own enough acreage that we could have a couple of horses.

YOURSELF

- I would have more free time to read in the evenings.

- I would lift weights when I wanted to because I would be working at home.

Exercise 2: Identifying the Positive and Negative Aspects of Your Life Today

In this exercise you will be developing two lists: one will contain the things that you like about your life now, and the other will contain the things you don't like. In composing these lists, use the same four categories as above. Try to think of all the things in your life that you may take for granted but that contribute to your happiness or unhappiness.

You will need quiet time to concentrate, a lot of patience, and brutal self-honesty to draw out the elements from your conscious and subconscious mind in compiling both lists. If you draw a blank, don't panic. The answer will surface. Being mindful of your reactions to people and things around you during your daily routine will help feed you ideas when you do the exercise. "Mindfulness, like creativity, is nothing more than a return to who you are. By minding your responses to the world, you will come to know yourself again. How you feel. What you want. What you want to do." So writes Ellen Langer, a professor of psychology at Harvard and author of *Mindfulness*.

For Example:

WORK
   THE POSITIVES

   • I earn a lot of money.

   • I enjoy what I do. It is challenging without being difficult.

   • I like the clients I work with.

   • Much of my work could be done at home.

   THE NEGATIVES

   • I hate the long commute to the office.

   • I dislike office politics.

   • I don't like being at the office until 6 P.M.

   • I don't like wearing business suits.

FAMILY AND FRIENDS
   THE POSITIVES

   • Our three kids go to private schools, and they take ballet, gymnastics, and karate.

   • We occasionally go sailing with friends.

   • We have season tickets to NFL games.

   • We go out to dinner twice a week.

   THE NEGATIVES

   • We never have time to entertain at home.

   • I can't spend as much time as I'd like to with my kids.

ENVIRONMENT
This includes where you live and work. Are you happy in your apartment or house, in the neighborhood, the city, the part of the country? Are having nearby video outlets and fast food restaurants a big plus for you? Are you crazy about the neighborhood deli? Do you like the nearby library, the ease of living in a condominium, the 20-minute commute to the ocean, the newsstand around the corner that has every magazine you could want?

THE POSITIVES

- The cost of real estate is escalating, giving me more equity in my home each year.

- I make more money here than I could elsewhere.

- There are a lot of cultural opportunities in this city.

- We love the restaurants here.

THE NEGATIVES

- Our neighborhood is getting unsafe. We see graffiti in the neighborhood, and we've been burglarized.

- The air is too polluted.

- We drive too much: to work, to drop the kids off, to shop.

YOURSELF
THE POSITIVES

- I'm proud of my family and our home.

- I'm successful at my job.

- I'm relatively healthy.

THE NEGATIVES

- I never read anymore.

- I don't get enough exercise.

All the reasons pro and con are not present to the mind at the same time; but sometimes one set present themselves and at other times another, the first being out of sight. To get over this, my way is to divide half a sheet of paper by a line into two columns; writing over the one 'Pro' and over the other 'Con.' Then during three or four days' consideration I put down under the different heads short hints of the different motives that at different times occur to me for and against the measure. . . . When each is thus considered separately and comparatively and the whole lies before me, I think I can judge better and am less liable to make a rash step; and in fact I have found great advantage from this kind of equation in what may be called moral or prudential algebra.

BENJAMIN FRANKLIN

Exercise 3: Focusing Your Objectives and Priorities
Now that you have listed the various items in the four different categories that contribute to your happiness or unhappiness, you need to focus on those that are most important to you. This exercise will help you figure out which item in each of your lists is most important, which is second most important, and so on.

Begin by evaluating each list separately. Compare the first two items on your first list and underline the one that is most important to you. Then compare the next two on your list, again underlining the most important one. After you have gone through your list, begin again, only this time comparing the underlined items and circling the one that is most important to you. After you have completed this exercise, consider those items circled. Depending on how lengthy your lists are, you may need to continue comparisons using some other identifying feature such as highlighting with a marker. Through this process of elimination, you will end up with the one or two most important items on your list—those which have been underlined, circled, and perhaps highlighted. These become the key objectives in that category.

For Example:

WORK:
THE POSITIVES

- I earn a lot of money.
- *I enjoy what I do. It is challenging without being difficult.*
- I like the clients I work with.
- *A lot of my work could be done at home.*

THE NEGATIVES

- *I hate the long commute to the office.*
- I dislike office politics.
- *I don't like being at the office until 6 P.M.*
- I don't like wearing business suits.

In the above example, the two key objectives (underlined and italicized) are the desire to work at home and avoid the long commute to work.

After you have identified the key objectives in each of the four categories, list them together under a new heading called "Key Objectives." Rephrase the items, especially if they are negatives, to read as positive objectives.

For Example:

WORK

- I prefer to work at home.
- I want to be able to get to work easily.

FAMILY AND FRIENDS

- I want to spend more time with the kids.

ENVIRONMENT

- I want to live where the air is clean.
- I want a safer environment.

YOURSELF

- I want more time to read.

These become your key objectives, which will help you decide whether or not to step off the fast track. (The number of key objectives in each category will vary with each individual.) Identifying and clarifying your objectives will make it possible to set up goals and, in turn, to develop a strategy and time frame for achieving these goals.

It may take a number of tries (especially if you are working this out with your spouse and/or family) before you find the proper order of things. The value of your list of key objectives cannot be underestimated, for it is the foundation upon which you will build your unique vision of happiness.

Exercise 4: Making the Big Decision and Setting Goals
The time has come to make the decision whether or not to get off the fast track! Most successful ex-FTers agree that it will be the most important, if not the most difficult, decision you will have to make.

Consider both your good life ideas (exercise 1) and your key objectives (exercise 3). Ask yourself, "Do I have this now?" "Is it possible to have this without changing my job?" "Is it possible to have this without changing where I live?" (Refer to chapter 7 for alternative solutions to quitting the fast track completely.)

If you find yourself having to choose between two good options, the next step is to use your good life ideas from exercise 1 and your key objectives as well as the other prioritized items from exercise 3 to see which option better answers those needs. This exercise will help you do a comparative analysis. The number of pros and cons will tip the balance in favor of one choice over the other.

As you list the entries under each of your options, give a value of 2 points to items that reflect your good life ideas from exercise 1 and key objectives from exercise 3; give other items a value of 1 point. (You may choose a different rating system to better reflect your prioritized lists, for example, giving key objectives 4 points, second most important items 3 points, third most important items 2 points, etc.)

In the following example, there are two possible solutions. The person could set up a home office and remain in the city, thus meeting four of the six criteria listed in exercise 3. However, one of this individual's key images for leading the good life (from exercise 1) is living in the mountains. Also, two key objectives (exercise 3) would require a move out of the city.

For Example:

HOME OFFICE IN CITY	HOME OFFICE IN MOUNTAINS
+2 Work at home	+2 Work at home
+2 Spend more time with kids	+2 Spend more time with kids
+2 More time to read	+2 More time to read
−2 Can't live in mountains	+2 Can live in mountains
−1 Still have traffic	+1 Less traffic
−2 Still have pollution	+2 Fresh air and blue sky
+1 Private schools	−1 No private schools
+1 More culture	−1 Fewer cultural opportunities
−1 Little outdoor recreation	+1 Lots of outdoor recreation
−2 More crime	+2 Less crime
+1 Earn more money	−1 Earn less money

After you have listed all of your entries and assigned them value points, add your two totals.

HOME OFFICE IN CITY   HOME OFFICE IN MOUNTAINS

Total Points: +1   + 11

The final tally should help you decide whether or not to step off the fast track. Other considerations will come into play as you gather more information from your research in upcoming chapters.

Now that you have brought your key objectives into focus and have evaluated what your best option is with regard to changing careers and/or relocating in order to realize those objectives, you need to write these things down in the form of *specific* goals. Identify them as short-term and long-term goals and list them in the order you plan to achieve them. In Lester Korn's book *The Success Profile*, Gary Wilson, executive vice-president and chief financial officer of the Walt Disney Company says, "If you know what you're trying to accomplish, and just kind of outline it in rough form, it makes the probability of achieving it that much greater."

For Example:

GOALS

1. Move to the mountains.
2. Set up a home office in new residence in mountains.
3. Spend more time with family, read more, and exercise more.

Take time to think long and hard, to question and evaluate what it means for you to live the good life. Are all the goals you have listed what you really want, or are any of them what others say you *should* want? One of the greatest of all achievements is to be able to break away from the dictates of others and to find the resources within yourself to define what is truly of value. If your dreams were to come true today so that you were doing what you say you want and had accomplished the goals you've just set for yourself, would you be happy?

If it is any help, imagine that your life is over and you're standing at the Pearly Gates. Will you have led the life you wanted to lead? Do the goals you've written above reflect that life fully?

Everyone's objectives change and evolve over time with changing circumstances in their lives. Repeat these exercises whenever you feel the need. Keep a dated record in your journal. It is a simple way to stay in touch with who you are and what you want from life. Your journal can serve as a great refresher for those difficult times when your goals seem unattainable.

Exercise 5: Making a Wish List

Your primary objectives are based on your primary needs. Then, there's your wish list—all that "pie in the sky" stuff! Your wish list consists of those things that you hope to someday have but that seem, at the moment, out of the question. As circumstances change, you may be able to move an item from the wish list to your list of attainable objectives. Having a wish list keeps you from thinking that your objectives are just dreams: you *dream* about your wish list; you *work* for your objectives.

Don Steinman always imagined someday organizing an authentic stagecoach drive across the desert. One day a favor was repaid him in the form of a vintage stagecoach. Steinman led his dreamed-of stagecoach drive, traveling over the mountains and through the desert, with a full team of horses and wranglers (and with plenty of media coverage along the way)!

> Do not spoil what you have by desiring what you have not; but remember that what you now have was once among the things only hoped for.
>
> EPICURUS

Bruce Neidermeier wished for a long time that he could sell his Christmas trees directly to customers and not be so dependent on his wholesale business. He set aside money when he could and slowly built a Bavarian-style outbuilding where he could set up his own "choose and cut" operation. He built large road signs, planted extra trees, and gave away hot cider and fresh popcorn. Finally he succeeded, and he now has customers coming directly to his farm to cut their own Christmas trees.

If you find that you are still uncertain about whether or not to step off the fast track, you may want to consider some of the alternative solutions discussed in chapter 7. However, if you feel that getting off the fast track is for you, read on to begin to make it happen.

DEVELOPING A STRATEGY AND TIME FRAME FOR MEETING GOALS

With your goals defined, you can plan a clearly defined strategy and a time frame for achieving both short-term and long-term goals. Chapters 4 and 5 will give you an outline of action to serve as a guideline. Although some ex-FTers did get out overnight, throwing caution to the wind and praying that fate would smile upon them, one of the key points of sound and effective management is that planning remains separate from execution. Spontaneity is, of course, a crucial factor in many success stories. Coupled with this spontaneity, however, was a fund of knowledge and experience that didn't leave much to chance.

In her book *Creative Visualization*, Shakti Gawain discusses a form of positive thinking in which visualization is used to help achieve goals. She offers the following four simple steps for effective visualization:

1. *Set your goal.* Decide on something you would like to work toward, realize, or create.

2. *Create a clear idea or picture.* Create an idea or mental picture of the object or situation exactly as you want it. You should think of it in the present tense, as already existing the way you want it to be.

3. *Focus on that picture often.* Bring your idea or mental picture to mind often, both in quiet meditation periods and also casually throughout the day when you happen to think of it.

4. *Give it positive energy.* As you focus on your goal, think about it in a positive, encouraging way. Make strong positive statements to yourself: that it exists, that it has come or is now coming to you. See yourself receiving or achieving it. These positive statements are called "affirmations."

Start Today

The first order of business is to decide what two actions you can take *today* toward meeting one short-term and one long-term goal. Set aside a few minutes to determine what two things you can do today. Decide that you *will* do these things, and then make the time to do them. As simple as it may sound, taking one step at a time *will* get you where you are going.

Francie Mishler never let a day slip by after she quit her fast-track career as an interior designer without learning something new about the herbal business she was planning to start (see chapter 5). She took a job at a floral shop, and she moonlighted as a waitress earning extra money to put into her business. She read every book she could get her hands on. She apprenticed with an individual who was knowledgeable on the subject of herbs.

> A thought which does not result in an action is nothing much, and an action which does not proceed from a thought is nothing at all.
>
> GEORGES BERNANOS

Larry and Mary Jane Barnes each worked two jobs during the years when they were getting their cycle touring business off the ground. Downtime was spent promoting, marketing, and advertising their business. Any extra money earned was put directly back into the business. After several years of working every day, they had moved into a position from which to make their dream come true.

Pat and Tom Garbrecht stayed at bed-and-breakfast inns whenever they traveled, learning all they could. They worked on renovating their own home, honing skills that they would eventually put to use when they opened their own inn. All the while, they continued to search for the perfect spot to open their business.

> Somehow, now, we have a lapse in initiative and the exercise of activity toward a goal. When people don't have an objective, there's much less dynamic effort, and that makes life a lot less interesting.
>
> BARBARA TUCHMAN

Learning all that you can about a future enterprise, saving money toward a future investment, and becoming more experienced and knowledgeable in your chosen field are all things you can do to meet short-term and long-term goals.

There is a wonderful feeling that comes with choosing *how you want to direct your life,* and then acting on your decisions. You will discover and relish this feeling at the close of every day that has brought you one step closer to meeting your objectives. You will discover what every successful ex-FTer discovered: the process *is* the adventure.

SUGGESTED READING

ALLEN, GAY WILSON. *Waldo Emerson: A Biography.* New York: Viking, 1981.

CANBY, HENRY SEIDEL. *Thoreau.* Boston: Houghton Mifflin, 1939.

DAVIS, CHARLES. *Harvest of a Quiet Eye.* Madison, Wis.: Tamarack Press, 1976.

DENLINGER, MARTHA. *Real People: Amish and Mennonites in Lancaster County.* Scottsdale, Pa.: Herald Press, 1975.

HOSTETLER, JOHN. *Amish Society.* Baltimore: Johns Hopkins Press, 1964.

JONES, RUFUS. *Quakerism and the Simple Life.* London: Headley Brothers, n.d.

PEALE, NORMAN VINCENT. *The Power of Positive Thinking.* New York: Fawcett, 1978.

PHILLIPS, MICHAEL, AND RASBERRY, SALLI. *Honest Business.* New York: Random House, 1970.

ROSZEK, THEODORE. *The Making of a Counterculture: Reflections on the Technocratic Society and Its Youthful Opposition.* Garden City, N.Y.: Doubleday, 1969.

_____ . *Where the Wasteland Ends.* New York: Doubleday, 1972.

SHI, DAVID E. *In Search of the Simple Life.* Salt Lake City: Peregrine Smith, 1986.

_____ . *The Simple Life: Plain Living and High Thinking in American Culture.* New York: Oxford University Press, 1985.

THOREAU, HENRY DAVID. *Walden.* Several editions to choose from.

TULKU, TARTHANG. *Skillful Means.* Berkeley: Dharma Publishing, 1978.

TZU, LAO. *The Tao Te Ching.* Translated by Gia-Fu Feng and Jane English. New York: Random House, 1972.

WHITSON, ROBLEY E. *The Shakers: Two Centuries of Spiritual Reflection.* New York: Paulist Press, 1983.

YANKELOVITCH, DANIEL. *New Rules: Searching for Self-Fulfillment in a World Turned Upside Down.* New York: Random House, 1981.

4

All you have in life is time. It's unknown
how much you've got, but how you spend it,
where you spend it, and with whom you
spend it is really up to you. . . . That's what
freedom is. (*Kansas City Star*, September 15,
1990)

SALLY VON WERLHOF-UHLMANN
Louisburg, Kansas

Exploring the Frontier: What to Do, Where to Go

PHOTOGRAPHER TURNED ENTREPRENEUR

Driving down Main Street in Silver Plume, Colorado—population 135
and an easy miss off the interstate if you are not watching for the road
sign—you feel as if a time warp has propelled you back to the late
1800s. The archaic structures stand in striking contrast to the sudden
majestic backdrop of the Rocky Mountains.

Tall blue delphiniums and pink, orange, and yellow poppies
take you around to the back entrance of what appears to be a century-
old hardware store. It is the residence of Gary and Joanie Regester and
their four children, Christian, Nicholas, Alexandria, and Rianna.

During the 1970s, Gary was a commercial photographer working
out of Los Angeles. Joanie was a commercial illustrator and designer.
Gary was known for his work with record companies shooting album
covers. Wanting a small-town atmosphere for their family, they decided to move to Silver Plume, which is west of Denver.

Since making the move, Gary has parlayed his photography experience and knowledge of backpacking equipment into his own business designing and manufacturing lightweight photography equipment for photographers shooting on location. His company, Plume Ltd., is known internationally for its exceptional, state-of-the-art photography equipment. Joanie takes on interior design projects that bring her to California on occasion.

Gary: I happened to go with the Nitty Gritty Dirt Band to the Soviet Union. All of the musicians were from Orange County but living in Colorado. I looked at being a photographer as an occupation not unlike being a musician in that you give a performance away from home. I shoot a job, deliver the film, and then I go home. I had enough of a clientele at the time that I figured I could freelance from anywhere in the country.

We weren't running away from Los Angeles. Both Joanie and I grew up in the suburbs and we knew that was what we didn't want. We thought we would be happy in either a metropolitan area or a small town.

When we started looking for a place to move we had certain criteria. We considered Seattle and Denver. Our number one criterion was mountains, although Joanie also wanted to be near the sea. Our second criterion was a centralized location in the United States, with easy access to New York and Chicago. That ruled out Seattle right away. Our third criterion was to be one hour away from an airport, and we found that here. In that respect, it's no different than when we lived on Fourth and La Brea in Los Angeles. We can fly directly nonstop to Europe from here.

We thought at the time that we could make our living commuting to an urban area. What happened was that we ended up living half the time in Los Angeles and here for two years before we could make the move. We kept the apartment in Los Angeles and then stayed with friends as we slowly made the transition to full-time residency. Our first baby was born in Los Angeles.

We finally made the cut in 1977. In 1980 I wasn't doing a lot of work in L.A. The bottom fell out of the record industry, and photography fees were cut in half. I'd been using part of my fee for airfare so now I couldn't do it anymore. In 1980 and 1981 we made $10,000 and we had two kids. There were moments when we were saying, "What are we doing here?"

About that time I was getting my business, Chimera [now Plume Ltd.], under way. I was designing and manufacturing soft-light equipment for photographers to travel with. It's funny, but the product I developed was an outgrowth of my having to travel from here to different cities to shoot jobs. I was getting work in different parts of the country because I was able to travel, be loose, and provide studio-looking shots. . . . At the time, we had made a commitment to just hold tight. Out of that perseverance and my ideas came this business, which has supported us ever since and is doing extremely well.

We don't miss the city because we are in the city at least once a month. We just returned from Europe with the whole family on a 21-day ticket. I was in Moscow recently for a week, then in Cologne, Germany, and I'm heading to Madrid on business. We try to take the children when we can. The school here works with us when we do that and gives the children homework to make up. I think the total time away has been a month so far this year.

The quality of the schools here is very high. There are just 300 kids in the elementary school, so they get a lot of attention. We know all the teachers personally, we know the school board members, and we run on government boards with many of them. Because of this additional outside involvement, parents have a lot of interaction with the teachers. I can't imagine that kind of interaction going on in the city.

I hear people argue that there is nothing for their kids to do here, and I don't understand. There's downhill skiing 15 minutes away from here, and my kids ski until June. The town just funded a recreational pool. The town has 40 kids, so my kids always have someone to play with. Until recently we didn't have broadcast television, and I preferred that, because I hate television. We used videos a lot.

I don't see any drawbacks whatsoever to living here. We are near an interstate freeway that gives us easy access to desired parts of Denver. We get to an airport in less than one hour—faster than people from Denver can get there. We are politically and socially involved. We have an extended family here.

The best advice I can offer to someone wanting to get out is to just do it. It's not as if you are giving up your talents and your brain and leaving them back in the city. You bring them with you.

We have a fax, a telex, five phone lines, an 800 number. We are not isolated. I have friends living in New York City who completely depend on their fax machines and phone lines. They don't go out much because it's not safe, for one thing. I am not any more isolated than they are.

In your attempt to answer the questions "What will I do for work?" and "Where will I move?" you will find a great deal of overlap involving a variety of issues, many of them affected by your spouse and/or family. For some, one question may take priority over the other. As you read through this chapter, take whatever information is applicable to your particular situation.

WHAT WORK WILL YOU DO?

In developing your vision of the good life in the last chapter, you explored the concept of choosing work that you want to do, with your work being a reflection of who you are. Some successful ex-FTers say that instinct played a major role in their decisions about what they would do for work once they quit the fast track. Instinct is defined as "an inherent aptitude or impulse." Most successful ex-FTers seemed to act on a combination of "instinct" and "intuition." In an article in *Psychology Today* (September, 1989),

> Responsible work is an embodiment of love. . . . We lose ourselves in our love of the task before us and, in that moment, we learn an identity that lives both within and beyond us.
>
> THEODORE ROSZAK

Nobel laureate Herbert Simon, professor of psychology and computer science at Carnegie Mellon University, said that "intuition is essentially synonymous with recognition." Intuition led some ex-FTers to recognize where their skills and talents lay, and to choose work they *wanted* to do rather than work they thought they *should* do. They chose to work at what they were good at, what came naturally—and that is where instinct came into play. In her book *Do What You Love, The Money Will Follow*, Marsha Sinetar writes, "It is as if they instinctively know what they must do with their time and energy, and then determine to do only that."

Again we are reminded of the significance of finding one's "right livelihood." In the *Briarpatch Book*, cited in *Chop Wood, Carry Water*, Michael Phillips describes the four qualities he believes are essential in choosing one's right livelihood:

1. Your work should be an area of great passion. Most of the time right livelihood means we get up and look forward to the day with the same excitement that we feel on vacations.

2. Right livelihood is something you can spend your life doing: this means the livelihood should have within it the room for your constant curiosity; it must give you room to keep learning, to grow in compassion; and it should offer you challenges that will try you and yet appeal to you time and again. Most livelihoods

actually have this potential, whether it is garbage collecting or systems programming, because the range of subtle and delicate refinements is always present.

3. It should be something that serves the community; you should feel that you are completely serving the community in what you do or you will have a longing as you get older to do something else and may have regrets. . . . But nearly every livelihood has enormous potential to serve people, and you will be serving people best when you are using your unique skills most fully.

4. And last, it should be totally appropriate to you.

> Do what you want to do, not what you think you should do. You'll never regret it. Once you start doing what you want to do, you become more in tune with yourself and have great confidence in yourself.
>
> Bruce Niedermeier
> *Wild Rose, Wisconsin*

If You Want to Keep the Same Career

Staying with the Same Employer.   This is most commonly accomplished by either getting a transfer to another office in the location of your choice or by setting up a telecommunications office at home in the new location.

Phil Guercio had been working for a brokerage firm in a large city on the West Coast. He and his wife had one child and were planning to have more, but they wanted to raise them near their extended families in Baton Rouge, Louisiana. Phil worked out an agreement with his firm to get a transfer to New Orleans, with the plan of working in New Orleans until an opportunity developed that would allow him to move to Baton Rouge. That opportunity came his way several months later.

> At the time, the move from California was costly. Although my firm was being accommodating by letting me transfer, they didn't feel obliged to help with moving costs. The other thing was that New Orleans was another big city that we had to go to before we could ultimately get home. Four kids later at "home" we see it was the right move. We have exceptional schools in Baton Rouge, the kids are growing up in the environment we always wanted for them, and Larke and I couldn't be happier being close to both our families.

Public Relations executive Victoria Houston was able to move to Connecticut while remaining employed by her company in Kansas City. She set up her office at home and uses a personal computer, fax machine, overnight delivery, and phone to continue her work. Houston travels to Kansas City approximately six times a year to do business in person.

SWITCHING EMPLOYERS.   If you are considering switching employers, ask yourself, "What does the employer in the area I want to move to need that only I can provide?" "What sets me apart from others equally qualified for the job?" The more you can convince a future employer that you are one-of-a-kind, the better your chances of landing the job. It is always better to meet a potential employer in person than to send resumes or talk over the phone.

Convincing a future employer that you will be a valuable asset to their business is best accomplished by demonstrating what a valuable asset you were to your former employer. Explain that you enjoyed and were successful at the work you did, and that the main reason you are changing employers is because of your desire to live in the new area.

People who know what they want and where they are going appeal to others because they appear intelligent, strong, confident, and sensible. You will most likely impress a potential employer if you share with them your idea of living the good life and how they fit into the picture.

Consider the possibility that the employer you most want to work for may not be ready to hire you for a year or more. Would you be willing to take another job until the position you want opens up?

Several months after Phil Guercio had relocated to New Orleans, he was offered a job by a regional firm in Baton Rouge. He had switched employers twice before he was able to move his family to the area he and his wife had originally set their sights on.

GOING INTO BUSINESS FOR YOURSELF.   Richard Gibbons used to work for a metropolitan home security company in Dallas. He still does the same kind of work, but he is now the boss of his own company outside Birmingham, Alabama.

If you are considering going into business for yourself, you might look to your former employer as a future client. Many ex-FTers start their own businesses and do consulting work or freelance projects for former employers. If you provided a special service to the company you used to work for, try offering the same service from your new location. Jon Goodson continues to work as a dairy nutritionist on Kellys Island, Ohio, acting as a consultant to his former employer. Carrie Stephanos quit her job as senior editor for a New York publishing house. She now lives in rural upstate New York and does freelance editing for the same publisher.

In recent years, telecommunications have made it possible for many former city-type businesses to operate from most anywhere in the country. Candace Berry was an executive with a national PR firm when she decided to go into business for herself. Living in the Vermont countryside has not affected her business. She says, in fact, that she has a surplus of projects from her several clients to choose from.

> With the work that I do, I can live just about anywhere. The services here are not as good as in L.A. but I've managed all right. In L.A. there are modeling agencies, prop houses, bookstores, and photo labs that I used. Some of the places still work with me and can send me stuff Federal Express. I have one sport place where I rent uniforms and props. . . . I can pretty well describe what I need over the phone and they Federal Express it to me the next day. . . . I started getting work from all over the country, so that really helped make it possible for me to leave L.A. Federal Express and a fax machine also made it possible.
>
> WAYNE WATFORD
> *Commercial Illustrator*
> *Phoenix, Arizona*

> Our direct marketing agency is connected all over the United States by telephone and fax machines. We've chosen to set up our business near Aspen, Colorado, because this is where we wanted to live and work. We can tolerate even the worst workload just because we love it here. Telecommunications makes it irrelevant where you decide to set up shop.
>
> DIRK KENNELLY
> *Aspen, Colorado*

Dozens of attorneys, stockbrokers, and accountants quit their firms in order to start their own businesses elsewhere in the country. Although some are able to get referral work from former employers, many make a go of it acquiring new clients in their new location.

Some ex-FTers continue doing the same kind of work but as supplementary income to a second career. This is a topic discussed further in chapter 5.

If You Want to Change Careers

More options exist for where you want to go if you decide to change careers completely (some people choose where to go as their top priority and then let that choice determine what they will do for work). If you are changing careers, chances are you are doing so because you are searching for work that will be more fulfilling.

Many fast-trackers in prestigious high-paying jobs are secretly frustrated chefs, woodworker, dog trainers, and biology teachers. Many spend their free time—what little of it they have—practicing the skills and talents that come naturally to them. When it occurs to them that perhaps they could make a living doing what they enjoy most, they often face self-doubt and the doubts of friends, business associates, and family members, who may tell them they're crazy or are just going through a mid-life crisis. However, for those who persevere, who believe in themselves and continue to strive and develop more completely, the time will come when they are able to act on their natural inclination. Proper stewardship of your talents and confidence in your skills will help you determine the type of work you will do off the fast track.

In his book *What Color Is Your Parachute?* Richard Bolles says, "The experts have discovered that . . . with job-hunting in general and career-change in particular, the more you can tap into your dreams the more you increase your chances of being able at last to do what you always wanted to do with your life." Tapping into your dreams can mean pursuing a field of endeavor for which you already may have not only prior knowledge and experience but also the necessary skills and talent.

Bruce Niedermeier, the Christmas-tree farmer we met in chapter 1, is skilled at working on the computer. His sideline work doing computer consultation is as much a hobby as it is a job. He also has leadership skills, which he discovered and developed in the army. It is the reason he is both good at and enjoys motivating the seasonal labor he hires to work his Christmas-tree farm. Further, he is a businessman; he spends his free time working up marketing packages because it's "fun." Finally, while in high school he picked up a lot of mechanical skills and worked a summer job as a maintenance person. As a result, today he is able to do his own farm-equipment maintenance.

Don Steinman, profiled in chapter 3, the former stockbroker turned wrangler, has a talent for and enjoys putting deals together and bringing different groups of people together. Where he once used to manipulate millions of dollars on the stock market, he now manipulates hayrides, horses, cookouts, stagecoach expeditions, and camp-outs for Wall Street hotshots, Girl Scouts, and whoever else might get a kick out of it. Where he once used to find tax shelters for the wealthy, he now has a four-bed bunkhouse for unemployed cowboys. Where he once used to throw $25,000 parties for social elite, he now cooks for wranglers on the ranch. Where he once used to employ his talents to make money, he now helps others share the kinds of things money can't buy—for example, a sky full of stars above a campsite.

Other successful ex-FTers find themselves doing a different but more enjoyable version of what made them a success on the fast track. Instead of designing layouts and writing copy for corporate clients, James and Carolyn Robertson now design and produce limited-edition handcrafted books at their Yolla Bolly Press in rural Mendocino County, California. Instead of working as a corporate attorney on Wall Street, Peter Moyer now works as a country lawyer handling local business needs in Jackson, Wyoming.

Sometimes being forced out of a job is the impetus some individuals need to pursue careers that are more in tune with what they really want to do. The shake-up on Wall Street at the end of the eighties redirected the lives of thousands. Scott Discount was highly successful on Wall Street, supervising the selling of different currencies at First American Bank. He was unexpectedly laid off when his employer shut down his trading desk. He now runs his own successful business, Scotty Wotty's Creamy Cheesecakes, using his mother's recipe and selling the cakes to gourmet stores in Manhattan.

Capitalizing on Old Skills, Acquiring New Ones.   If you have a variety of job skills, you have that many more avenues to follow up. Be imaginative in your search for employment. Job skills that successful ex-FTers employ are not always the skills they have been educated in. Many are skills picked up in their younger days—working as a tradesman to get through college, working in the family business during high school vacations, working at a hobby for the simple pleasure of it.

A personal hobby is quite often a source of skills, knowledge, and experience that can be turned into a career. Poul Jorgensen, whom we met in chapter 1, is a classic example. He has made a full-time career out of fly-tying. Larry Barnes capitalized on one of his hobbies, bike-touring, when he started his Rocky Mountain Cycle Tour company. Gary Regester used his knowledge of backpacking, a hobby of several years, to develop lightweight photo equipment.

There are a variety of ways to acquire knowledge and experience in different fields of work without having to go back to school full-time. One way is to work for someone else and learn a business. Francie Mishler, who you will meet in chapter 5, worked for free part-time for an herb-grower and craftswoman until she had learned all she could about starting up her own herb-growing business.

Another way is to take a short-term course or attend an apprentice-program to learn a trade or a craft. Charles Fuller learned blacksmithing in this way. Whatever the field of work you are considering, go to your local library and do some research on what is available to get you started. Richard Bolles's Manual for career changes, *What Color Is Your Parachute?* is an excellent resource book on the hundreds of different career options available.

How will you know if a career is going to be right for you? How will you know if you can be a success at it? When I was a student at Amherst College, I once asked the question "How will I know if this is the right direction for me?" of Benjamin Demott when he was teaching there. Without hesitation, he responded, "You will know because you go after it with a ferocity unlike anything else in your life. The ferociousness carries you through the worst of times." In his book *The Power of Myth*, Joseph Campbell often refers to this "following one's bliss":

> We are having experiences all the time which may on occasion render some sense of this, a little intuition of where your bliss is. Grab it. No one can tell you what it is going to be. You have to learn to recognize your own depth. . . . When I taught in a boys' prep school, I used to talk to the boys who were trying to make up their minds as to what their careers were going to be. A boy would come to me and ask, "Do you think I can do this? Do you think I can do that? Do you think I can be a writer?" "Oh," I would say, "I don't know. Can you endure ten years of disappointment with nobody responding to you? . . . If you have the guts to stay with the thing you really want, no matter what happens, well, go head."

People who love their work tell you it is an extension of themselves—an instinctual obsession. If they don't yet have the formal training or the necessary experience, they are driven to get it. And people who love their work and are really good at it never stop learning about their craft, their business, their profession, their art. They strive to be the best at what they do.

> Tom is a chemist and I'm a nurse. For years, we've stayed at bed-and-breakfast spots all over the country whenever we had a chance. We learned all the pros and cons. We knew that as soon as we could afford to, we would start our own.
>
> We took a seminar for starting up a bed and breakfast, and we ended up answering most of the questions from everybody because we knew all the answers! There isn't one facet of this business we weren't already familiar with.
>
> After four years of looking we found the perfect spot in an area we loved with the nicest people. Tom had restored our 100-year-old house in Lancaster, so he knew exactly what to do to restore this beautiful stone house. I love to cook and take care of things. Starting up this bed and breakfast was a chance to do what I think we are really good at.
>
> PAT AND TOM GARBRECHT
> *Bed-and-Breakfast Innkeepers*
> *St. Germaine, Wisconsin*

PREPARING FOR YOUR NEW WORK BEFORE YOU MOVE.   Whatever you plan to do for work, be certain you are prepared to do it *in advance of your move*. Have your qualifications, accreditation, and licenses in order—whatever is required for you to set up shop. This includes preparations for supplemental income. For example, if you think you can teach part time but don't have the accreditation, take the time to become qualified; if you think you can work as a tradesmen or a contractor, be sure your license and/or qualification is up to date.

If you plan to take up work that has not earned you an income before (even though it may have been a hobby), you should acquire the fundamental expertise necessary for that line of work. This is not the time to come in as a neophyte if it might jeopardize your family's welfare. Hoping to earn a living as a watercolor artist without ever having sold a painting isn't just risky—it's stupid. In contrast, having immersed one's mind, body, and soul into a craft or art or trade or business for a good part of one's life and, as a result, having developed an expertise in that field is legitimate reason for seeking to earn a living at it on one's own. Experience and skill change what appears to be a risk into an opportunity.

An important issue to keep in mind if you decide to go into business for yourself is supply and demand. Will you have a market for what you are selling? Many successful ex-FTers depend on clients outside their new communities. Anthony and Susan Stevens grow organic vegetables on their farm in Martinsburg, West Virginia, and sell some of their produce to elegant restaurants in Washington, D.C. Don Steinman does a fair amount of business with Wall Street executives who come to his Tucson dude ranch for their vacations. (Being able to sell your skills or products in the area you plan to move to is a subject we will investigate later in this chapter.)

Have a Backup Option

What if the work you want to do won't be possible to do right away? Perhaps you have to wait for the local judge to retire; or you plan to buy the local florist business when they sell in two years; or you have a year to wait before joining a local law practice. Whatever the delay, it doesn't prevent you from taking part-time or temporary work to hold you over. Many ex-FTers depend on their additional job skills to bring them work while they wait for their "regular" job to pan out. Don Smeller, a qualified civil engineer, moved with his family to Wenatchee, Washington. After three years in the area, he has yet to find the professional work for which he is highly qualified. He has the job skills of an electrician, however, and is able to work as a tradesman.

Larry and Mary Jane Barnes (whom we met in chapter 1) worked as a carpenter and a part-time travel consultant, respectively, until their cycle-touring business was able to bring in enough income.

Christian Andrade began delivering newspapers to make ends meet until he and his wife's bed-and-breakfast operation got under way.

Bruce Niedermeier could not earn enough money his first years farming Christmas trees and supplemented his income teaching and working part time as a computer consultant.

Francie Mishler worked as a waitress for a few years until her herbal business could finally stand on its own. She slowly cut back her work hours until she was waitressing only Saturday nights before making the final break.

In some instances, ex-FTers decide to continue their part-time work even after their regular work is doing well. They do this because they enjoy it and also because the part-time work offers nice supplemental income to their primary job.

Michael Powers quit his job as a systems computer analyst and took on two jobs to make ends meet. Today, he still works a full-time job as an auto parts salesman and also works part time as a dairy farmer because he thoroughly enjoys it.

> I get up at 5 A.M. to milk the cows and I'm at work at the auto parts store by 8 A.M. I love it. My life has never been better. I left the computer business seven years ago. . . . I make a third of what I used to earn and that's just fine with me. . . . I have free time now that I never had before.

WHERE WILL YOU LIVE?

Let your personal vision of the good life guide you. Let it be the foundation upon which you build your investigation of possible places to move. Your vision includes a blueprint of those key objectives having to do with your work, your family and friends, your environment, and yourself that you most want in your life. Whether you have a spot in mind or not, it is a good idea to do the research and have at least two backups—two additional places to consider in the event that your first choice doesn't work out.

In the first part of this section, you will take a look around various parts of the country to help you narrow down your selection. The second part will help you choose some likely spots in those areas using a variety of considerations as a guide. The final part will offer advice on how to familiarize yourself with a location you are considering.

Many of us have a dream of where we would love to live and work. Too often, however, people rule out the places of their dreams before they even begin their search. The notion of compromise has frequently been drilled into us to the extent that we don't believe we can actually have what we want, but must settle for something less. Give your dream free reign, and at least consider the possibilities!

Narrowing It Down

If you were given a chance, this very moment, to move to any part of the country, where would you choose to go? The mountains in Idaho? The desert in Arizona? The lake country in northern Minnesota? The quiet countryside of rural Vermont? Would you like to live in Santa Fe, New Mexico? The town of Clearfield, Pennsylvania? Somewhere off the coast of Maine?

Many successful ex-FTers had prior knowledge of and experience in the areas they wanted to move to, having become familiar with them in different ways:

SOME GREW UP OR SPENT TIME THERE AS A CHILD.   Ellen Kimble grew up in Marfa, Texas. She had lived and worked in Burbank, California, more than 20 years before deciding to move back.

Robin Ogden left Los Angeles for Minneapolis where she had grown up.

Phil Guercio, mentioned earlier, left the West Coast, then left New Orleans, to return to his hometown of Baton Rouge, Louisiana.

Bruce Niedermeier, the Houston accountant turned Wisconsin Christmas tree farmer, had grown up in Wisconsin and attended the University of Oshkosh, although his wife Lori had never been to Wisconsin.

Wayne Watford and his wife moved back to Phoenix after spending time with her family there.

SOME LEARN ABOUT A NEW AREA WHILE ON VACATION.   Don and Sandy Smeller became familiar with Wenatchee, Washington, while on their camping trips to Lake Chelan.

Christian and Lea Andrade first learned about San Juan Island after taking a weekend vacation there.

Kirstie Wilde and her husband Paul Miller had vacationed in Pacific Grove, California, and then later decided to move there.

Peter Moyer and his wife had a vacation home in Jackson, Wyoming. They came to know the area while skiing in the winter and fly-fishing in the summer.

SOME LEARN ABOUT AN AREA THROUGH THEIR WORK.   Eleanor Hopkins learned about the area around Hilton Head, South Carolina, after spending a three-day weekend there for a company convention.

Jody Rush was familiar with Texas, having worked there after she graduated from college. Years later, she left her job in Washington, D.C., in order to live and work in Austin, Texas.

Scott Orazem, a fashion photographer, is considering buying property in Arizona, which he learned about while shooting on location there.

Some Learn About an Area Through Their Hobbies and Special Interests.   Poul Jorgensen decided to move to the Catskill Mountains because of his interest in fly-fishing.

Marsha and Harold Gold are avid collectors of Indian pottery. After several trips back and forth between New York and New Mexico, they decided to move to New Mexico.

But what if you have little knowledge or experience of other parts of the country? This was my own situation. My husband Todd and I decided to travel by car across the country and look for potential areas to move to. We took these trips as our summer vacations for three years in a row. Three different times we thought we found what we were looking for—once in northern California, then in Central Oregon, and then, finally, near the Sawtooth Mountains in Idaho. However, as it happened, before we could return to Idaho for what would have been our third visit, we discovered the small farm on a lake in northern Wisconsin where I had grown up. Having family nearby had a great deal to do with our finally choosing Wisconsin over Idaho.

Sue Smoot is another example of an ex-FTer who had little knowledge of where she wanted to move. She had narrowed it down to western instead of eastern United States, but that was all. She took time off from work and spent several weeks driving through several western states until she determined that Taos, New Mexico, would best suit her needs.

Driving through various regions of the United States is a luxury that many cannot afford because of time and/or money. But there are other ways to become generally acquainted with different parts of the country before you actually begin your research into specific counties, cities, towns, or rural communities.

The best, most up-to-date resource material can be found in Richard Boyer and David Savageau's *Places Rated Almanac: Your Guide to Finding the Best Places to Live in America* and also their *Retirement Places Rated.* They are both excellent sourcebooks for answering questions you have about different parts of the country regarding climate and environment, cost of living, work opportunities, recreation, housing, health care, education, and even personal safety.

Any library reference desk can help you become familiar with different regions of the country and can be topic-specific if you tell them what your primary interest is (for example, work or environment).

> We left California because their sales tax is brutal to the small businessman. We looked into Nevada—they are the best, the most attractive to any entrepreneur starting up, and we looked into Arizona.
>
> BOB AND KATIE MARTIN
> *Lake Havasu, Arizona*

Other resources include travel and tourist bureaus, newspaper travel sections, real estate companies, and a wide variety of magazines and books that offer regional information. A day spent browsing at your local bookstore or library can get you well enough acquainted that you can at least pick out a few states to consider. Please refer also to the appendixes at the back of this book for lists and maps showing different climate regions, earthquake and tornado zones, and nuclear power plant distribution.

The next step will be to choose a few counties in the states of your choice and to begin more specific research. In the appendixes, I recommend what I think are the best locations to move to in the United States. These "ideal counties" can be seen on the map in appendix A and are listed alphabetically by state in appendix B. I have selected these counties using various criteria. Most important, they are a combination of the best suggestions from successful ex-FTers and some of the best recommendations from Jack Lessinger, professor emeritus of real estate and urban development at the University of Washington at Seattle. Lessinger, who is the author of *Regions of Opportunity,* has done extensive research in real estate across the country. He has earmarked ideal regions to move to, classifying them as a whole as "Penturbia":

> Penturbia exists in almost every state. It's the sleepy little hick town, the scenic spot, the rustic community free of the shopping centers, vast parking lots, and manicured lawns that characterizes suburbia. . . . It includes counties with a humble present but a promising future: counties where an acre can often be bought for as little as a thousand dollars, where population is beginning to pour in, where property values are starting to rise. And where a long-term shift in migration signals that the rise will continue for many decades.

In making my selection of the best counties in the United States, I have also used specific criteria gathered from the most recent edition of the *County and City Data Book*. These criteria include limited population size, less costly real estate, close proximity to outdoor recreational areas, above-average number of physicians per number of residents, high socioeconomic status, and above-average number of households with incomes of $50,000 or more (often indicating a high number of college graduates and professionals).

Put more simply, I have attempted to focus on areas where you can find clean air, blue sky, a nearby hike into the country, real estate you can afford, good schools, good health care, an economic base that will be friendly to new business, and the possibility of meeting someone like yourself.

Once you have chosen a state or region of the country that interests you, choosing counties within that area can be a hit-or-miss proposition. I recommend that you pick a half dozen or more counties in the area you are considering, call at least one chamber of commerce in each county, and ask to have whatever material is available sent to you. This is a simple task to do. Appendix C provides addresses and phone numbers for all state chambers of commerce. The state chamber of commerce can give you numbers for local chambers of commerce in the counties you have selected. They may give you a specific city or town. Most chambers of commerce will send you information on surrounding areas or communities, so don't worry about getting too specific. You are merely getting a taste for and adding to your knowledge of the area.

It can be very exciting to assess the material arriving in the mail from places you are interested in. This preliminary research will help narrow your search to even more specific choices. When you receive the information, if you decide it is not what you are after, you are that much closer to deciding what you *do* want. *The easiest road to discovering what you most want is discovering what you don't want.*

If nothing appeals to you in this first roundup, try another region of the country.

Choosing a Likely Spot

Do you have a picture in your mind of where you would like to live? What are the chances of being able to do the kind of work you want to do and earning a reasonable income there? Again, try running wild with a few ideas before you settle down to practical considerations.

Be certain to include your spouse and any family members in this initial research. Including them at the outset will ensure that it is everyone's move, not just your own.

Your decision to move to one area instead of another may mean the difference between earning a comfortable living but not being able to buy the property you want, or between living on the edge but in a spectacular environment, or between living close to family but with little cultural opportunity. It is therefore important to stay as close as possible to your vision of the good life as you begin making choices. An article in *Mother Earth News* (January, 1987) quoted Gary Beverly and his wife Molly who experienced some of the trade-offs.

> We wanted to live on some beautiful, remote acreage as self-sufficient potters and gardeners. We knew we'd need money and more skills to make it, so we looked for jobs and were lucky enough to find one at a community college in Prescott [Arizona]. We put our savings into a house on an acre in Chino Valley, a tiny farm town 16 miles north of the college, and settled in to learn the area. Initially, we didn't like what we found: the growing season was short, the wind was incessant, salaries were low (especially for women), and the whole place seemed to be about 15 years behind progressive, innovative, youthful Santa Barbara. We quickly returned to the West Coast, bought 16 acres in Northern California, and began commuting 1,000 miles, one way, for two years to do basic development work on our beautiful, remote, little hollow. We came to know the problems there, too: the cold, the distance from urban markets, the heavy competition, and the high costs. This taught us a valuable lesson: No place is perfect! It's where your head and heart (not your body) are that counts. In the end, we sold the California place and made our stand on five acres in Arizona.

The purpose of this section is to help you focus on exactly the kind of place that will meet your requirements. Refer to the exercises you did in chapter 3 and the lists you now have in your journal. Consider the goals you set for yourself. Include your list of imagined ideas of the good life, your list of set goals, and your wish list (you never know when something unexpected might become possible!).

Study the material you have gathered so far. In this preliminary research phase, you will need to take a number of elements into consideration:

Work Opportunities

Business Services

Environment and Climate

Real Estate

The Community

Education and Culture

Recreation and Leisure Activities

Medical and Other Services

In the pages that follow, we'll consider each item in turn. Make a list in your journal of the questions that are relevant to your particular circumstances, along with any others that come to mind. This list of questions will come in handy when you begin talking with contacts in the area you're researching. In covering each consideration, keep in mind the priorities of the objectives you developed in chapter 3.

Work Opportunities

- Will you need to rent or buy commercial property for your work? (Also see the upcoming real estate section.)

- What resources are crucial for you to do the work you want to do? Suppliers? Distributors? Wholesalers? Part-time employees?

- Does your work require that you be close to an airport or an interstate freeway, or be within commuting distance of a city?

- Does your work depend on a strong local economy?

- Will you depend on local clients? Does the size or character of the city/town/rural area affect what you will do for work? Will it affect the demand for what you are trying to sell—your expertise or any products?

- Are you planning to supplement your income with part-time work, a temporary job, or a sideline business? What will you need in order to do so in this locality?

Perhaps you want to practice dentistry part time in Hood River, Oregon, so you can raise your family in the country and spend your free time board sailing, or you find that the area around Sedona, Arizona, inspires the watercolor artwork you do when you're not working as a designer. What opportunities are there for dentists in Hood River, and designers in Sedona?

The first order of business is to *find someone doing exactly what you want to do*. There exists no more valuable resource. Ask anyone and everyone if they know somebody doing this work in this kind of place. If you are a professional looking for work, it is an excellent idea to talk with other professionals in the area you are considering. There may be a small law firm eager to invite you in because of your expertise. Perhaps a local accountant, stockbroker, or dentist is planning to retire and is looking to sell the practice. If possible, go see this person. A personal interview can elicit the kind of information you can't get over the phone. (This is something that falls under the next main section, on familiarizing yourself with your chosen area, and should be done after the initial phase of research by phone and mail.)

> I had arranged to talk with three local dentists. One fellow gave me very bad advice about setting up my practice in one of the outlying incorporated communities that didn't even have electricity! This was an older fellow who, I think, resented new dentists coming into the area. The other two I spoke with were very helpful. One has since become a good friend.
>
> DR. JOHN CLARK
> *Eastern Nebraska*

If you're planning to switch careers and start up a new business, begin by talking to the experts in your field. This applies whether you want to farm ginseng root, start a recycling center, restore Cobra race cars, collect and sell antique Coke machines, or set up a millinery shop. Remember, no question is too stupid! Quiz them on their accounting methods, their suppliers, how their families like the business, the drawbacks, their dumbest mistakes, their most memorable successes. If you are polite, honest, and straightforward about why you would like to talk to them, the majority will respond favorably and feel complimented to be asked for advice. Interview more than one person doing what you want to do wherever it is they live.

Don't hesitate to talk with others doing your type of work in the community you plan to move to, even if you think you pose a competitive threat. It is better to know this going in. Be open and honest about your intentions. You will want to gather as much information as you can regarding the supply and demand for whatever it is you are selling. Keep in mind that the more expert you are at a job and the more skills you have, the better your chances will be at finding a market for what you hope to sell. A crucial question to ask yourself is, "What can I offer to the local community that they don't already have?"

> Many people make the mistake of projecting the vitality of the city onto the rest of the country. In many small towns, it can be a terrible problem finding a job. You don't see want ads for professional people in the local newspaper. (Los Angeles Times, March 3, 1989)

To get the names of people who might be able to advise you, call (again) the local chamber of commerce. Tell them what you are interested in doing and ask their advice. Is there a need for a bed and breakfast? Is there someone in a similar profession they could recommend you call? Ask them to refer you to one or more real estate people in the area. Most people, when they hear they have been recommended by their local chamber of commerce, will be flattered and more than happy to answer a few questions. When you phone them, there is no harm in inviting them to breakfast or lunch on the day you plan to visit—or just for a cup of coffee, if they are too busy for a meal. The added plus of making these contacts is that you will have made your first friends in town, and the value of this cannot be overestimated!

In the event that you strike out with a local chamber of commerce—there may not be one, they may not be terribly helpful, whatever the reason—go on to try another information source, such as a local real estate company, a church organization with which you are indirectly affiliated, a community college information office, or other such resource. Be creative—you never know who can provide answers to your questions or direct you to someone in the community who can be of help.

Resources

Call the local or regional office of the Small Business Administration. They will refer you to a SCORE (Service Corps of Retired Executives) counselor who may be able to advise you in your endeavor or refer you to someone who can.

Call the local chamber of commerce for referrals.

Order a copy of the local telephone book and yellow pages to find experts in your field.

Subscribe to the local newspaper.

BUSINESS SERVICES

- What resources are essential for operating your business?
- Will special equipment need servicing?
- If your clients are out of town, are there specific transportation or shipping needs?
- What will it cost to use outside suppliers?

Will you have access to the suppliers, the distributors, and services you need to do your work—for example, gourmet wholesalers, printers, government offices, automotive suppliers, shipping companies, rental machinery, and temporary employees? It is very easy to take for granted the countless resources in the city. In some areas you may choose to relocate to, you could discover that there is no one to repair the fax machine. Make a list of the key ingredients that allow your business, trade, craft, or service to function.

Example: Advertising Agent for Professional Artists

WHAT I NEED TO FUNCTION

- Telephone: Private line (no party line)
        Call waiting
        National and international long-distance access
        Telephone credit card capability
- Office equipment: Fax machine
            Computer and printer
            Typewriter
            Answering machine
            Xerox machine
            Disks, paper, and printing supplies
            (Repair facilities)
- Delivery/Postal: Overnight delivery (second-day won't do it)
- Nearby airport: Not more than an hour away

- Office supplies: Foam core, illustration board, 4 x 5 and 8 x 10 transparency sleeves, mounting boards, portfolio cases, and the like

- Photo studio: To copy artwork 4 x 5 and 8 x 10 format

- Photo lab: To develop color transparencies overnight

- Shipping: UPS

- Newspapers: *LA Times, NY Times, Wall Street Journal* Delivery same day

- Trade publications: *Adweek, Ad Age, Workbook, Blackbook, American Showcase,* and so on

- Local post office: Bulk mail shipments

Although the list above is relatively simple compared to a business manufacturing a product or a franchise feeding dozens of customers, it poses problems for the individual who wants to live in an isolated or rural area where the roads might be washed out in a storm and deliveries hindered. Repair facilities pose another challenge. How long will the computer be down before it can be serviced? Arrangements would have to be made for out-of-town photography and lab capabilities. Portfolio supplies would have to be ordered and shipped from a metropolitan area.

Katie and Bob Martin manufacture model airplanes. In 1983, they moved their operation from Los Angeles to Lake Havasu, Arizona. The Martins did their homework before heading out of the city. They knew they would need a reliable trucking outfit to ship their model airplanes throughout the country, and they knew they would always be dependent on hard-to-find materials. Before moving to Lake Havasu, they researched and discovered two or three reliable trucking companies. They could not, however, resolve their supply needs and made up their minds in advance to plan a trip once a month to Los Angeles to buy the difficult-to-find machine parts. Since relocating, they have worked out arrangements with shipping companies to get the things they need in a timely fashion.

David Kimble, an internationally known commercial artist working out of Burbank, California, considered relocating to Marfa, Texas. He depends on local labs in the city to provide him with oversize film positives that he paints on. He communicates daily with his assistants and is dependent on local photographic services throughout key phases of production. He knew he could communicate with his assistants using the telephone and a fax machine, but his need for lab and photographic support created an insurmountable problem.

Ray and Melissa Perez were interested in starting up an authentic Mexican restaurant in Eagle River, Wisconsin. They soon discovered that the expense of fresh lettuce, tomatoes, chilis, cilantro, corn, tortillas, and so on in the dead of winter was cost-prohibitive: they would not be able to compete with the fast-food competitors just down the block.

Scoping out the local area to find what resources may or may not be available will spare you future headaches.

Will the local economy support your profession or your business?

Carla McDougall wants to run an espresso and French pastry sidewalk cafe with a side gourmet catering business. She knows she needs to be in an area with year-round sunshine and year-round disposable income. That means tourists. She learned from experience to be wary of company towns. If the company is raided by a Wall Street junk bondsmen, her little business will feel the impact. So she is scouting out tourist communities with a healthy economy not at the mercy of Wall Street.

Finally, be aware that if you are moving to a depressed area you must be prepared to take a large cut in income, since there will be a limit on how much you can charge for whatever you are trying to sell to the community.

Resources

Contact the local chamber of commerce. If they are a member of the American Chamber of Commerce Researchers Association (ACCRA), they will be able to provide you with a general cost of living for your area, including the cost of housing, food, transportation, health care, and services.

Visit your local library and look up the most recent edition of the *County and City Data Book*. It will give you raw statistics on a wide variety of subjects, including population, annual household incomes, house and land values, and so on, for the particular area you are interested in.

Call your long-distance operator to order the 800-number directory.

For AT&T try: 1-800-426-8686
For MCI try: 1-800-444-4444
For IT&T try: 1-800-441-6665

Once you order the directory, you can call national suppliers, vendors, wholesalers, and the like, to find out whether they service the area you are moving to.

Order the yellow pages and/or the local telephone book to find the resources you may need.

Call the local chamber of commerce if your needs are more specific. If they can't help you, ask them to refer you to someone who can.

Home-office books, specific business books, and trade books, among others, can help you to determine inventory needs if your business is new.

Environment and Climate

- Do you want to be in a smaller city? A small town? A remote rural area?
- Will you need to be close to a city? Will you need to commute? How long a commute are you willing to make?
- Does your outdoor recreation include the ocean? The mountains? The desert? Lakes or rivers?
- Do you want to be near wildlife refuges? National and state parks?
- What kind of climate do you want to live in?
- Do potential energy costs pose a problem for you?
- Are you interested in owning acreage? A ranch? A farm?

When you move to an area where your livelihood depends on the environment, you're living the rains and the heat and the wind. You realize you're dependent on Mother Nature. Out here, you just roll with the punches.   (*Kansas City Star*, September 15, 1990)

Joe Gregg
Beloit, Kansas

What kind of environment do you picture yourself in? Will your goals require a certain kind of physical setting? Some ex-FTers depend on a particular physical setting for their livelihoods. Larry and Mary Jane Barnes operate their Rocky Mountain Cycle tours in Canmore, Alberta—spectacular, scenic country that is a must for attracting cycle tourers. Sue Smoot operates a bed-and-breakfast inn in Taos, New Mexico, a setting that appeals to tourists. Don Steinman found "cowboy country" in the desert of Tucson, Arizona, where he operates his dude ranch and riding stable. Bruce and Lori Niedermeier bought into an existing Christmas-tree farm in central Wisconsin— they purchased land that is sandy and bad for most crops except Christmas trees, which thrive in the area. The Dixons set up their fishing lodge on a world-class salmon-fishing river in Alaska.

Hundreds of other ex-FTers migrate from one physical setting to the next, following the seasons and the tourist trade. They operate businesses that cater to the tourist trade, such as clothing retailers, restaurateurs, and arts and crafts dealers.

> A cloudy day, or a little sunshine, have as great an influence on many constitutions as the most real blessings or misfortunes.
>
> JOSEPH ADDISON
> *The Spectator*

If your livelihood does not depend on the scenery, the land, or the climate to attract business, your choices for where to live are limitless. Beware of romantic influences from the advertising industry. Remote, inaccessible acreage in Wyoming is not necessarily "Marlboro Country." Buying property in the middle of Iowa farm country may not be as cheery and inviting as the McDonald's commercial would have you believe. Be realistic in your assessment of the surrounding area and give careful consideration to the weather.

One of the primary reasons people leave a new area is because they cannot acclimate to the weather. Urban dwellers are accustomed to working indoors, traveling on well-maintained freeways, and insulating themselves from bad weather. You need to be aware that moving to rural America or even to a smaller city in a completely different climate might mean muddy roads, freezing pipes, problems getting your car started in subzero weather, endless rainy days, or 100-degree summers. This might suit you, or it might not.

> For the man sound in body and serene of mind there is no such thing as bad weather; every sky has its beauty, and storms which whip the blood do but make it pulse more vigorously.
>
> GEORGE GISSING
> *The Private Papers of Henry Ryecroft*

And if you do move to a rural area, is this the clean, safe, healthy environment you want to raise the kids in? No contaminated ground water? No toxic dump sites? No nuclear power plants in close proximity?

What are the energy requirements: the cost of oil, gas, electricity, and water? If you don't have natural gas, how much is it going to cost to have it piped in? What was the oil heating bill for last winter? Fuel and electricity for the home were two of the fastest rising costs on the Consumer Price Index in recent years.

A visit to the area of your choice during the off season will be the best way to discover if the climate and environment suit you (more about this later).

Resources

See maps in appendix A.

The United States Department of Commerce has a local Weather Bureau office with complete weather information for every county in every state. Call information for the local number or write:

U.S. Department of Commerce
Weather Bureau, Climatological Section
National Records Section
Asheville, North Carolina 28801
Phone: 704-259-0682

The local airport and fire department will have accurate weather statistics.

Contact the local utility company for average monthly costs.

Ask the seller of the property you are interested in to provide you with sample monthly energy bills (you will need to balance seasonal costs).

Real Estate

- What kind of home do you want? For instance, are you interested in a four-bedroom house in town or a small cottage on a lake? Do you want a ready-to-move-into house in an upscale neighborhood, or a fixer-upper outside of town?

- If you work out of your home, will you need extra office space or an outside workshop?

- Are you looking for commercial property?

The price of real estate is usually relative to the size of the nearest city or town and the state of the economy there. Before you visit an area, ask a local real estate agent to send you a current listing of the types of property you are interested in and ask for photographs if they are available.

> We worked with three different real estate brokers and canvassed the area for four years looking for the perfect spot [bed and breakfast]. We wanted it to be right the first time. We didn't want to hope for something better down the line and have to start all over again.
>
> TOM AND PAT GARBRECHT
> St. Germaine, Wisconsin

Donna and Jim Onstott, whom you will meet in chapter 7, recommend using a small local real estate company instead of the larger, nationally franchised agencies, which may be out of touch with the kind of property you are looking for.

> Starting about three years ago, [the Onstotts] began looking in earnest for a lot of 20 to 30 acres within 40 miles of downtown Minneapolis. They consulted brokers from a few of the large, nationally franchised real estate agencies with offices in the area. "They either laughed at what we could afford, or else they showed us some things that were totally inappropriate. Then, when we were driving on back roads one weekend, we stopped at a teensy agency. Right away, they showed us three or four properties, all of which were better than anything the bigger realtors had shown us." They bought one of those properties: a 28-acre parcel with an irregular, south-sloping meadow surrounded by a dense hardwood forest. (*Harrowsmith*, March, 1988)
>
> DONNA AND JIM ONSTOTT
> Hudson, Wisconsin

Resources

The section in this chapter on familiarizing yourself with an area will offer some basic information on looking for property. This is not meant to be comprehensive, of course; there are dozens of national and regional books dealing with the purchase of real estate— what to look for, how to protect yourself, and so on. The books I found most helpful include:

Les Scher's *Finding and Buying Your Place in the Country*
Robert Nessen's *The Real Estate Book*
Mark Levine's *The Field Guide to Home Buying in America*
Hollis Norton's *How to Make It When You're Cash Poor.*

The Community

- Are you interested in a college town?

- Does the character of the community make a difference to you?

- Are you interested in continually meeting new people such as in a resort community?

- Are you looking for a small metropolitan area big on cultural events?

- Do you want a more traditional small-town atmosphere, one that has changed little over time?

The smaller the area, the more you will want to know about the inhabitants. Some people who have moved to the hinterlands have discovered that they have absolutely nothing in common with the locals, and they end up feeling isolated and lonely. You might consider subscribing to the local newspaper for a few months—it will capture the community's personality.

> In an urban setting, relationships are mostly secondary to activities. In a rural environment, relationships are primary: Everyone knows everyone else. . . . It's more laid back in a small town, but that dramatically affects privacy. . . . There aren't necessarily window-peekers around, but a new person is an oddity and becomes the topic of conversation. . . . Churches offer more than just religion. They're the center of entertainment in many small towns. . . . Friday-night softball, Saturday-night dinners, and Wednesday-night bingo can be very popular. If you don't go to church, you're viewed with suspicion, not because you're considered godless, but because people will wonder what you do with yourself when you're not working. (*Wall Street Journal*, "Managing Your Career," Supplement 1990)
>
> Douglas Bachtel
> University of Georgia

Religion and politics are a concern not often looked into by prospective residents. However, not only should you find out whether the church or religion of your choice is represented, but you will need to know whether there exists an atmosphere of religious or racial intolerance.

Several years ago, Derrick Reasley bought acreage outside Fairfield, Iowa. He loved the idea of small-town America, and he was especially attracted to the growing population of transcendental meditators. He had no idea he was in Bible Belt country, and that the TM followers (few, if any, of whom were natives) were an unwelcome bunch in the local community. After a couple of unfriendly episodes, he sold his property and moved back to the city.

Will your political beliefs be diametrically opposed to those of your new neighbors? A classic example is that of well-to-do, environmentally concerned people who move from the city to a rural area, then demand a no-growth policy to preserve the pristine look of the countryside. They want more property set aside for preserves. They want to halt the harvest of timber. They want to protect the wildlife. Many of the locals, however, earn their living in the construction business: they need to harvest the timber, run their sawmills, cut their roads, build new homes . . . and consider the pesky city slickers to be unwelcome outsiders.

> One problem I see with outsiders who come in is their hurry to get too involved right away. They are too eager to make changes right away. Wait and let us see you for a couple months before you become too familiar. There is a passage in the Bible I think where it talks about the newcomer taking the less honorable place at the table and waiting to be asked up to the front.
>
> GARY REGESTER
> *Silver Plume, Colorado*

Resources

Subscribe to the local newspaper (be sure to read the editorial page). Ask to be put on the mailing list for church bulletins, the arts council, and other local organizations.

EDUCATION AND CULTURE

- What kind of schools will your children be attending?
- What quality of education are you looking for? What extracurricular activities? What sports facilities?

- How good is the local school system?
- Are you or your spouse interested in attending a community college or university to continue your education?
- What sorts of cultural offerings are you looking for?

Are there nursery schools? Private or just public schools? Some of the very best schools are public schools in small communities where small class sizes allow for more individual attention. Look into the quality of education before you discount any institution. What do the junior high and high school offer in foreign languages, sports facilities, extracurricular activities? Is there a junior college? A university? The latter two can be of special importance if you are continuing your education, changing careers, or looking for personal enlightenment.

Rural cultural activities are, as a rule, different from those in the city. You may find yourself participating rather than being an audience. Square dancing may replace ballet. Folk music may replace the orchestra. The rodeo may replace Yankee Stadium. Ask around, "What do folks do for fun around here?" Local church organizations can help you find out what goes on. There is nearly always a local arts council. Call up the president. Most outsiders are happily surprised to discover the network of art, dance, music, and literary activities flourishing in even the most remote communities. The Regesters, for example, participate in the annual musical "melodrama" featured every spring in Silver Plume, Colorado, a town of 135. Members of the community help build sets, design and sew costumes, and write and produce the play, which draws attendance from as far away as Indiana. If you choose to move to a smaller city, you will more than likely have big-name, mainstream cultural offerings every bit as rich and varied as in a larger city.

Resources

The Rating Guide to Life in America's Small Cities by G. Scott Thomas. Call the local chamber of commerce for educational and cultural information.

Recreation and Leisure Activities

- What will you and your family spend your free time doing?
- What outdoor recreation are you interested in?

- What hobbies? What special interests? Do your hobbies or outside interests require special materials, equipment, suppliers?

- Do you want to be near a health club? Gymnasium? Pool? Golf course? Racquetball court?

- Will you want access to a library? Concert hall? Stadium? Theater?

If you plan to move to a rural area, you may have a big change in how you spend your leisure time. Are you a sports enthusiast? Keep in mind that your own sport may not be represented in your new town: for example, a rural area will likely have no racquetball courts, no Olympic-size indoor pool, no year-round tennis, no golf. How dependent are you on video outlets? Fast-food chains? Jazz radio stations? Ethnic restaurants? Perhaps you like to drive an antique or foreign car. Will you be able to get parts and servicing?

> Any time you need an out-of-the-ordinary item, it has to be brought in by special order. "If your car is laid up in Orange County, no problem. . . . Here they call around and call around and finally locate a part in Reno. Then there's a snowstorm in the mountains, and who knows when the truck will get in." (*Los Angeles Times*, March 3, 1989)

Do you spend your free time growing orchids, breeding dogs, collecting antiques, playing viola with a string quartet? It's important to find out whether your favorite activities will be doable.

> We tried living in the New Hampshire countryside for two years. Our closest neighbors were 20 minutes away. After a while it just got plain boring. When you are accustomed to city living and having so many things to do, it feels like you have entered a vacuum. We decided to move back to the city.
>
> PEGGY AND JONATHON OLSEN

Resources

Call the local chamber of commerce.

Check the local yellow pages and phone book.

To learn more about recreational opportunities in our national parks, forests, and wildlife refuges, write to or call:

Department of the Interior
National Park Service
Office of Public Affairs
Public Inquiries
P.O. Box 37127
Washington, DC 20013-7127
Phone: 202-208-6843

Department of the Interior
Fish and Wildlife Service
Publications Office
1849 C. Street N.W.
Washington, DC 20240
Phone: 202-208-5634

Department of Agriculture
National Forest Service
Publications Office
201 14th Street S.W.
Washington, DC 20250
Phone: 202-447-3957

Medical Services

- What are your medical needs? (Does any member of your family require special medical attention? Are you planning a pregnancy?)
- How close is the nearest hospital?
- Is there a trauma center in case of an emergency, and is there ambulance service?
- Are there medical specialists in the area?

Many of these questions can be answered with a single phone call to the medical community (local clinic or hospital) in the place you've chosen.

Resources

Your local library would have a copy of the American Hospital Association's annual *Guide to the Health Care Field*. It is organized by state and city and lists addresses and phone numbers for local medical facilities. It will provide you with all the information you need regarding specialized facilities, certification, ownership, and so on.

If you still have unanswered questions regarding any of the categories above, you can call General Reference at the Library of Congress, phone: 202-707-5522. They have a state-of-the-art data base and can assist you on any subject.

Familiarizing Yourself with the Place You've Chosen

WEEKEND IT.   All of your research until now has been over the phone and by mail. The time has come for a visit. Even a weekend will do. It is a good idea to bring your spouse and/or family for reasons mentioned already. Approach it as you would a weekend vacation. Relax and enjoy yourself. This doesn't have to be "it." You want a general feeling for the area and that means allowing for a little spontaneity.

On our trips cross country, Todd and I were open to participating in a local activity if we happened on something of interest. On one occasion in Idaho, we came upon a field trial competition for Labrador and golden retrievers. We spent the afternoon thoroughly enjoying ourselves, and made the acquaintance of a half dozen local residents. On another occasion, we attended a local firemen's pancake breakfast somewhere in Montana and felt very welcomed.

> Denver is different from parts of Maine or Vermont, where you're not going to become an insider unless your grandfather was born and raised there. I think in any place it helps a lot if you know someone before you move there. If you have one or two contacts.
>
> GARY REGESTER
> *Silver Plume, Colorado*

Try out the local restaurants, stop by a softball game, see what's going on at the park, the beach, the local library. Strike up as many conversations with the locals as you can to ask them about the area. You might want to stop and see the local junior high if you have a son or daughter that may be attending it.

> Look at movie theaters, restaurants, shopping centers, and bars. Talk to people there and ask what they like about living in the town. Remember . . . you're not going to Ethiopia. All of your needs will be met, but life definitely will be different. (*Wall Street Journal*, "Managing Your Career," Supplement 1990)
>
> DOUGLAS BACHTEL
> *University of Georgia*

You may run into natives who dislike outsiders, are bigoted against ethnic groups or religious persuasions, despise city slickers, or are just unfriendly. Not all people in a small town think alike, however, and before you give a place the thumbs down, try to see its more pleasant side. Have a beer at the local tavern or coffee at a popular breakfast stop and you may gather a little insight. Try to listen and observe—they'll guess you are from out of town anyway.

MAKE A SECOND VISIT.   Once you've spent a weekend in the location and liked what you found, go back for a longer visit—preferably in the off-season. See Montana's bleak winters, get to know the oppressive summer heat of southern Arizona, check out a 40-below-zero week in northern Minnesota. Better to get the surprise over with. Reading about it or having someone warn you is not the same as being in the middle of it.

The longer you visit, the better a feeling you can get for the place. This may be difficult for many who may not be able to get time off from work, or are unable to coordinate time off with a two-income family, or find it difficult taking children out of school. You might consider asking for an unpaid leave of absence from your job if you have set money aside to cover expenses (more about this in chapter 5). You could legitimately tell your employer that it is for family reasons. Or, you might be able to try a "flex-time" work schedule so you can put in extra hours to get a three-day weekend. If your family didn't accompany you on your first visit, plan to take them along this time.

When you talk with the local residents, tell them about your plans and needs. Someone may give you the lead you need to find a job, buy a home, start a business, or convince the family!

An important attitude to assume once you begin talking with the locals is that you consider yourself a future asset to the area—someone who will contribute to the betterment of the community: you are not arriving here merely to take advantage of cheap real estate and the recreational opportunities.

INVESTIGATE WORK OPPORTUNITIES.   Your first order of business is to set the wheels in motion for earning an income. A number of free-lancers—such as many writers, artists, and consultants—have the luxury of being able to work just about anywhere. If this is not the case for you, find out whether what you are selling—professional services or expertise, consumer goods, craftsmanship—has a market in the immediate area or in the surrounding communities. Is there a small city within reasonable driving distance? Is there a way of testing the local marketplace before fully committing? Is there a business like yours that you might approach for a little advice? Can you set up a temporary moonlighting operation that would require monthly visits? If you need office space, now is the time to price leases or rents. Any job resources that you will be dependent on should be investigated. If what you need isn't available, find out what the alternatives are. Work out the logistics of what it will take to set up an income-producing operation.

Both Sue Smoot and Christian and Lea Andrade returned to their chosen places for a longer visit to do a "feasibility report." Would their plans for work succeed? In both cases, this extra footwork gave them the confidence to go ahead as planned.

If you are looking for a particular job in the area, fill out job applications and set up job interviews. Try to contact all potential employers. Follow every lead you scared up during your initial research. Leave no stone unturned. Work is found through knowing somebody, or through a friend of a friend. Laying the groundwork for your future livelihood will be the largest task you undertake. Diligence and thoroughness at this stage of the game will pay immeasurable dividends in the long run. Don't forget to send a thank-you to anyone who offered help during your visit. (Besides being a polite thing to do, sending a thank-you reminds the person of your job search!)

LOOK FOR REAL ESTATE.   Before you arrive for your second visit, set up an appointment with a local real estate agent who can show you around. (On your first visit, you may introduce yourself to a few local agents and see if there is someone you prefer, then arrange for a second visit.) Also, ask whether the agent can recommend someone for you to talk to regarding your work, since real estate people tend to know a great deal about business in the town, the small city, or the rural area you are interested in. You may have many questions to ask about the local housing market, especially the cost of renting (in chapter 5, I strongly recommend that you rent before buying property once you relocate). Be very specific about your needs with the agent. What is winter access like? How efficient is road maintenance during bad weather? If you don't find what you are looking for with one real estate agency, try another. You may also want to simply drive around and see for yourself what is for sale and for rent in the community.

There are many things to consider before buying property, some of them not so obvious. Among the considerations are the following (and see chapter 5, the section titled "Moving—with Caution"):

EVALUATING STRUCTURES

- Compare to other houses or buildings in the neighborhood. The price may reflect the value of the area rather than the actual worth of the structure.

- Examine placement of the house in relation to privacy, views, sunlight, the environment in general. If the house is surrounded by trees, imagine what winter will be like with the additional dampness.

- Examine the interior. Do the floors slope? Are there water stains on the ceiling? Are there cracks in the wall? Is there corner rot in the bathroom or kitchen? Is the plaster or paint peeling? Is there telltale termite, carpenter ant, or beetle debris? Check for recent plastering, painting, and taping that may be disguising a fault. Is there evidence of wood rot? Are storm windows or double-pane glass needed?

- Is the house or building connected to public sewage lines? If it has a septic tank, when was it installed and how often did the former owners need to have it pumped? Ask abut the electrical, heating, and air-conditioning systems. Is the house heated with oil—a potential money drain if you have to make the conversion from oil to gas. Has the fireplace been used—ask to see it in action. How well insulated is the house?

- You might want to hire a professional inspection service to point out the faults in any structure. Ask for a bid to do the inspecting. You may use the inspection to affect the selling price.

LEGALITIES

- Familiarize yourself with easement and water rights. Mineral, oil, gas, timber, soil, and other rights may or may not be relevant.

- What are taxes and insurance on the property?

We started looking throughout the Sierra foothills. It was before Prop. 13 and we knew we'd get eaten alive by property taxes if we lived anywhere in the near vicinity of the Bay Area.

James Robertson

- Are property lines verified? Is there any possibility of an adverse possession suit with the neighbors?

- What are the zoning requirements? Will they prevent you from turning a single residence into a duplex?

- What other state and local laws may affect you? For example, homestead laws:

Buy where homestead laws preclude the possibility of losing your house to finance companies or banks. For information on home-steading in each state, contact the Bureau of Land Management (BLM) Land Office in that state.

Anonymous Stockbroker

PROXIMITY

- How close is the airport? The interstate freeway? The fire station? The nearest grocery store? Schools? Is there mail delivery? Utility services? Medical center?

Be sure to have an outside expert or two evaluate the land, the house, and/or the commercial building, before you go into escrow. And keep in mind that neighbors can sometimes be more helpful than the "experts"! Talk with the next-door neighbors and ask them to walk the property lines with you. Don't be afraid to make stringent demands on the seller about anything in question (for example, well-water suitability, septic capability, property line disputes). Find out whether the new freeway they plan to build will cut through the acreage next door. Is there a beetle blight in the forest adjoining your backyard?

ACQUAINT THE FAMILY

You've got to have a strong marriage—starting a new life somewhere else is a difficult thing. We had no friends when we moved here. (*USA Weekend*, September 14, 1990)

BILL RAUCHES
Beaufort, South Carolina

Familiarize your family with the area and see what needs can be met. Is there a junior girls' swim team? A local chapter of the Sierra Club? Are there weekly folk concerts? Does the rodeo come to town? A 4-H club can be an eye-opener for pinball-jaded city kids. If you are relocating to a smaller city, you will find many of the same offerings that you had in a larger city.

One obstacle to overcome that may affect you, your spouse, and certainly your children is anxiety about adjusting socially, meeting new friends, and feeling at home in a new area. This takes time. The best you can do for reluctant family members is to be reassuring and to find an interest for every member of the family so that the transition will go more smoothly. Family members can then begin to look forward to what's ahead rather than focusing on what they are leaving behind.

A FEW WORDS OF ADVICE

If you begin to feel bogged down by the research, the phone calls, the homework in general, it's a clue that what you are after may not be what is going to make you happy. Successful ex-FTers say they loved doing the footwork, making plans, seeing the whole process as an adventure. This isn't to say that it's all easy, but this is, after all, supposed to be your dream.

A note of caution, and optimism: Many people consider throwing in the towel with their first wave of bad news (often, they had cold feet from the start and were waiting for an excuse to back out). But if you have been sincere, and you have gotten this far, don't let a bad break deter you from your quest. Sleep on it, then do some more homework. Give your dream a 110% chance. Worse than trying and failing is to be haunted forever by the thought, "But what if I had . . . "

SUGGESTED READING

BERRY, WENDELL. *The Gift of Good Land.* San Francisco: North Point Press, 1981.

BOLLES, RICHARD. *What Color Is Your Parachute?* Berkeley: Ten Speed Press, 1990.

BOYER, RICHARD, and SAVAGEAU, DAVID. *Places Rated Almanac: Your Guide to Finding the Best Places to Live in America.* New York: Prentice Hall, 1989.

_____. *Retirement Places Rated.* New York: Prentice Hall, 1987.

FIELDS, RICK, et al. *Chop Wood, Carry Water*. Los Angeles: Jeremy Tarcher, 1984.

GILDER, GEORGE. *The Spirit of Enterprise*. New York: Simon and Schuster, 1984.

HAWKEN, PAUL. *Growing a Business*. New York: Simon and Schuster, 1987.

KIRKPATRICK, FRANK. *How to Find and Buy Your Business in the Country*. Pownal, Vt.: Storey Communications, 1985.

LESSINGER, JACK. *Regions of Opportunity*. New York: Times Books, 1986.

LONG, CHARLES. *How to Survive Without a Salary*. Toronto: Summerhill Press, 1988.

MAY, ROLLO. *Man's Search for Himself*. New York: Dell Publishing, 1953.

NEARING, HELEN and SCOTT. *Living the Good Life*. New York: Schocken Books, 1970.

PHILLIPS, MICHAEL. The Briarpatch Community. *The Briarpatch Book*. New Glide/Reed, 1975.

SINETAR, MARSHA. *Do What You Love, The Money Will Follow*. New York: Dell Publishing, 1987.

THOMAS, G. SCOTT. *The Rating Guide to Life in America's Small Cities*. Buffalo: Prometheus Books, 1990.

5

If one advances confidently in the direction of his dreams, and endeavors to live the life which he has imagined, he will meet with a success unexpected in common hours. He will put some things behind, will pass an invisible boundary . . . he will live with the license of a higher order of beings. . . . If you have built castles in the air, your work need not be lost; that is where they should be. Now put the foundations under them.

HENRY DAVID THOREAU

Planning for Your Move

INTERIOR DESIGNER TURNED HERB GROWER

Twenty minutes south of Akron, Ohio, is the small town of Canal Fulton, where Francie and John Mishler have their "Catnip Corner Herb Farm" on seven acres. They grow hundreds of different herbs, which they sell for culinary and decorative purposes (and an occasional homemade remedy). She teaches classes in the decorative use of herbs and offers tours of her gardens to small groups. She sells to customers throughout the country.

> My love of plants started when I was a kid. My mother always had gardens. There were five of us kids, and we were always made to participate. I remember cutting fresh flowers and arranging them when I was in the seventh or eighth grade.
> I had a career as an interior designer for more than five years. I had to dress up every day and spend long hours at the office. Just being inside a building drove me crazy. I longed to wear my jeans and work in the garden. During this time, my husband and I purchased seven acres in the country and held on to it until we

could afford to build. We both wanted desperately to live in the country.

I had given the thought of quitting a lot of consideration. I had a pretty good idea that what I most wanted to do was work with plants and preferably work outdoors. I knew I could always get a job working as a waitress to hold me over until I could get a small business going. I got up the nerve and quit my interior design job. The day I quit, my boss called me into her office and asked me if I didn't want to someday own a beautiful home and own lots of nice things. I said I could have a very nice home and not have to work at a job I found stifling. I immediately started waitressing and working part-time in a local floral shop.

While I worked at the floral shop I was maybe too much of a perfectionist, but I think I've always had a lot of pride in seeing a job well done to the end. And I had this feeling that I ought to be the boss! I finally decided to quit and start my own business. All the while I continued waitressing.

Then an interesting thing happened. My sister and her husband are antique dealers. Around the corner from them lived an older woman named Ruth who had beautiful herb gardens. Her house was done very much in the Shaker tradition, and she made elegant herbal wreaths. As soon as I met her, I asked if I could work for her for free all summer if she'd teach me her trade. She agreed, and every Monday for the whole summer I weeded her gardens, made wreath bases, and learned a lot of what she knew. She kept giving me starts of this herb and that—a start of oregano, a start of thyme—and I planted them in my garden at the seven acres where we now lived. I read every book I could get my hands on about the subject.

Ruth even taught me about marketing. She worked different craft shows. The largest in the country, the Yankee Peddler, is on for three weekends in September, and 65,000 people a day go through it. I worked the trade show with Ruth, and we dressed in costume and demonstrated our craft. On the second weekend, I decided to try to sell a few little bundles of my own herbs from my garden. My husband laughed and said nobody would pay money for them. Well, I sold them all! I did it again the following weekend with even more bundles, and I again I sold them all. I expanded my garden the next year, and this time I took wreaths to the craft show. Every one of them sold!

In 1984 I opened my own shop on my property in a little building that had been there when we bought the land. It had no electricity, no dry wall, hardly anything, but it was old and charming and small. All the money I earned from my business I poured right back into the business. I continued waitressing on the side. I had set a fixed amount of money I had to earn, and I wasn't going to quit until my business could make it on its own. I waitressed another two years, slowly cutting back until I was just working Saturday nights. That's one piece of advice: persevere, and don't let what anyone else says bother you—including your spouse! I have gotten negative responses all along and have loved proving those people wrong.

I work an average of 12 to 15 hours a day, but I enjoy it. My husband is a workaholic as well, and he helps me out. My business comes to me strictly by word of mouth. It has grown so fast that I'm now faced with the prospect of going direct mail, and I'm not sure I want to get any bigger than I already am. I think I'll keep it small—I don't want to become an administrator!

I love my business. I love being on my knees in the dirt in my garden. Everything I wanted to do, I'm doing.

FRANCIE AND JOHN MISHLER
Herb Growers
Canal Fulton, Ohio

CORPORATE ATTORNEY TURNED COUNTRY LAWYER

At dawn every weekday morning, Peter Moyer feeds his daughter's pony, bundles his three children into the Jeep, and drives eight miles through the valley at the base of the Teton Mountains to drop them off at school. By 8:30, he is at his desk in a bare, two-room law office across the street from the courthouse in the center of this town of about 5,000 people. After doffing his parka, the lanky, 42-year-old attorney removes his shoes, tucks in his denim work shirt and gets down to business as one of the town's most prominent lawyers. . . . In 1981, he pulled the plug on his promising career as a top Wall Street lawyer and headed for Wyoming. His new life, he says, is every bit as good as the dream. (*New York Times*, March 25, 1990)

Peter and Robin Moyer don't complain about the years they spent on Wall Street and their life in New York City. They were relatively happy, in fact, and enjoyed the work they did. He was headed for a partnership at a prestigious law firm where he had met Robin, a paralegal. He and his wife had a new baby and discovered the difficulty in raising a child in the city. They thought there could be a better life for themselves and their baby elsewhere and after thinking about it for a year, they decided to get out.

We started looking around New England. We were interested in Maine and also in Stowe, Vermont. We thought at one time about running a country inn. We had a vacation home in Jackson, Wyoming—a ski place where we had honeymooned. There was something about the West, a wildness that we didn't have in New England. We just up and moved into the vacation home and lived there for five years before selling it and building our new home.

We have three kids now. I take the oldest to school, about an eight-mile drive from home. The second-oldest goes to the Montessori school, which is right around the corner from my office. I have a lot more time for fishing, hiking, and cross-country skiing, and enough mental energy left over from work to read a book. In the city, you spend so much time on business that you're lucky to get through a comic book on the weekend!

I think what I did at the time was actually risky. I had no carryover work from New York. Very little referral and that was the scariest part. I had no idea if I was going to make it here as a lawyer.

The West is a lot friendlier place than the East in general, I think. You have to adjust, though, and slow down. New people come into town wanting to run things. Big-city arrogance annoys the old-timers. There has been an ongoing clash for years between the old and the new. The old guard have their way of doing things and you have to try to fit in. Since coming here Robin and I have both become a lot more active in the community. Since she works full-time as a real estate agent, she is affected by the emotional issue of how many more people are moving here.

We really have the best of both worlds. In a resort town like this you have folks coming in from back East and from Europe, so there is a lot of diversity.

Don't get me wrong—this is not Shangri-la, and there is a lot less money to spend. But what you're buying here is blue sky, and a lot of what you want is free. It's been hard, but we don't have any regrets.

PETER AND ROBIN MOYER
Lawyer and Real Estate Agent
Jackson, Wyoming

PUTTING YOUR FINANCES IN ORDER

By now, you probably have a pretty good idea of where you want to go and what you want to do. Let's assume you are not independently wealthy, a recent winner of the lottery, or about to inherit the family winery. What you are plotting to do involves risk.

As noted earlier, while many successful ex-FTers claim they simply got out, the majority actually had the following in common: they began planning their departure at least six months in advance; they were familiar with the area they were planning to relocate to and its people through personal contact; they knew what they would do for work; and they had enough money to live on for one year. Many had also sharply reassessed their financial situation and spending patterns in preparation for stepping off the fast track.

Budget for Your Goals

A good place to begin putting your finances in order is eliminating your consumer debt. Set up a time frame for paying off any credit card debt you have, budgeting for the maximum you can afford to pay monthly. Consumer debt, especially debt spent on perishables such as entertainment, airline tickets, meals, gas, and groceries, is the worst kind. You end up paying a lot more for these things long after their purchase. From now on, write checks for all perishables.

> The cost of a thing is the amount of what I call life which is required to be exchanged for it, immediately or in the long run.
>
> Money is not required to buy one necessity of the soul.
>
> HENRY DAVID THOREAU

> I left the fast lane for a more tranquil lifestyle. Money just isn't that important to me any more. I earn enough to pay my bills and have what I need left over. I'm not in debt. I tore up my credit cards a long time ago.
>
> POUL JORGENSEN
> Catskill Mountains

CHART CURRENT EXPENSES, AND TRIM THEM.   If what you need is very similar to the lifestyle you are currently living, you may not be ready to exit the fast track. If you truly want to get out, you will automatically have to come down a couple of notches in lifestyle, at least for a while—that's a given. Decide what you need to survive. To discover what your real needs are in preparation for stepping off the fast track, begin by scrutinizing what you currently spend money on. Chart a few months worth of past bills and expenses to see clearly your pattern of spending habits. Be as thorough as you can—no item is too small to mention. Set up a chart similar to the following example in your journal, and fill it in. Account for every expense: lunch at the deli, gassing up the car, movies on the weekends, racquetball court rental, health insurance, birthday gifts, and so on.

Here is an example of one family's record of expenses for three months:

The Wilsons are a family of three. Kathleen Wilson works as an editor for a newspaper and earns $55,000. Her husband, Peter, is an executive with a publishing house and earns $60,000. They have a son in high school. They own a house in Amherst, Massachusetts.

Clothing	July	August	September
everyday:	—	$ 250	—
work clothes:	—	—	$1400
schoolclothes:	—	—	$ 350
extras:	$ 300	—	—

Credit cards			
total monthly payments:	$ 450	$ 450	$ 450

Education			
monthly tuition:	—	—	—
school supplies:	—	—	$ 100
lessons:	—	—	—

Entertainment			
dinners, parties:	$ 155	—	—
movies:	$ 50	$ 50	$ 50
video rentals:	$ 15	—	—
outings:	$ 80	—	$ 45
books, magazines:	$ 35	$ 40	$ 25
TV cable:	$ 55	$ 55	$ 55

Food			
groceries:	$ 500	$ 500	$ 500
eating out:	$ 200	$ 200	$ 200

House			
mortage (rental):	$1200	$1200	$1200
property tax:	(included in mortage)		

House (cont.)

home repairs:	$ 145	$ 75	$ 20
home supplies:	$ 30	$ 25	—

Insurance

health:	covered		
disability & life:	$ 250	$ 250	$ 250
house:	(included in mortgage)		
car:	$ 175	$ 175	$ 175

Medical (covered)

unexpected:	—	—	—

Miscellaneous

pets:	$ 50	$ 75	$ 50
church, charity:	$ 75	$ 75	$ 75

Phone

	$ 120	$ 150	$ 140

Taxes (monthly)

state and federal:	$2300	$2300	$2300

Transportation (2 cars)

gas:	$ 45	$ 60	$ 50
carwash:	$ 20	$ 20	$ 20
car payments:	$ 450	$ 450	$ 450
maintenance:	$ 40	$ 315	—
		(timing belt)	
miscellaneous:	$ 10	—	—

Utilities

oil/gas:	$ 35	$ 40	$ 50
electricity:	$ 45	$ 50	$ 55
water:	$ 20	$ 20	$ 25
Totals:	$6850	$6825	$8035

An average monthly overhead based on the three months charted above comes to approximately $7,200 a month. There are various ways to trim this budget. For each item, ask yourself whether there is a way to change or eliminate the need. Be rigorous. Mutual agreement among family members is important.

If you chart your expenses every month, you automatically become attuned to each purchase. Every time you attempt to buy something frivolous, the specter of your chart will haunt your conscience. Every expense cut from the chart means money in your pocket. Wash your own car. Cut back on long-distance phone calls. Eat at home more often. Get your heels resoled rather than buying new boots. These monthly "savings" tally up for a total that can be very rewarding. Think of the money saved as money toward your new life. Just as important, the savings are a way of measuring how well you are doing at making a change in your lifestyle.

ESTIMATE YOUR FUTURE INCOME AND BUDGET.   The next step is to develop a ballpark figure of what you expect your future income to be. In the example above, the Wilsons are planning a move to the Midwest, where Kathleen will work for a smaller newspaper and expects to earn $40,000; she also plans to moonlight as a consultant and hopes to earn an additional $5,000. Peter is planning to start his own business as a book packager and estimates his first year's income at $20,000.

It is also necessary for you to forecast your financial position for at least a year. Here's an example of how tricky things can be: The Wilsons are planning to sell their principal residence and buy a less expensive house in the Midwest. This is referred to as "buying down" and has implications for paying capital gains taxes. Consider the following likely scenario: Let us assume the Wilsons sell their home for $300,000. They owe a $120,000 mortgage. They pay $25,000 to improve the house within 90 days of its sale and they pay a 6% real estate fee to the agent handling the sale. They pay an additional $2,000 closing costs. The house they will buy is $150,000. The IRS says that if the purchase price of your new home is less than the adjusted (this means you subtract the additional money spent to sell the house) sale price of your old home, and you buy and live in the new home within two years, the capital gain will be determined by the lesser of two factors: 1) the gain on the sale of the old home; 2) the amount by which the adjusted sales price is more than the purchase price of the new home. In the case of the Wilsons, factor 2 applies: the difference between the adjusted selling price of $255,000 ($300,000 − $45,000 = $255,000) and the price of the new house, $150,000, comes to $105,000. At 28% (beginning in 1991), the capital gains tax comes to $29,400.

Thus:

1. They sell their home for $300,000.

2. It costs them $45,000 to sell their home.

3. This gives them $255,000, out of which they pay their mortgage of $120,000, leaving them with $135,000.

4. They pay $150,000 cash for a new home. Deducting that price from the adjusted sales price of the old home gives a capital gain of $105,000, which at 28% equals $29,400 they owe in taxes.

5. Therefore, they will have $135,000 − $29,400 = $105,600 to put down on the new home.

If they pay cash, they will need an additional $44,400!

This is a hypothetical, bare bones example to help homeowners estimate how capital gains tax will affect their financial position. It is an important issue to resolve for many ex-FTers who plan to buy down—purchase less expensive homes in their new location. It is why I strongly recommend getting financial counseling (discussed later in this chapter) as you make your financial estimates.

> My advice to most people coming in is not to come in under-capitalized. In general, you are better off with a cushion after you buy into a retail business or whatever you are planning to do. You need enough to get you through the hard times, at least one year. And there are hard times. I was lucky—my practice started to do well a lot quicker than I thought.
>
> Peter Moyer
> Jackson, Wyoming

Once you have a fix on the amount of income you will be able to generate in your new environment, the task of cutting back expenditures will become easier. In your journal, set up a budget of estimated expenses based on your future income, and always budget a surplus to cover the unexpected. If you view your budget as a way to develop good habits rather than to regiment your life, it will have a far greater chance of succeeding. Again, using the Wilsons as an example:

LIVING EXPENSES

(Average per 3 months)	*Fast Track*	*Good Life*
Clothing	$ 760	_____
Credit cards	$ 450	_____
Education	$ 30	_____
Entertainment	$ 235	_____
Food	$ 700	_____
Housing	$ 1300	_____
Insurance	$ 425	_____
Medical	0	_____
Miscellaneous	$ 130	_____
Phone	$ 140	_____
Tax	$ 2300	_____
Transportation	$ 645	_____
Utilities	$ 115	_____

Income
  (yearly)

Salary	$115,000	$ 60,000
Interest income (not adjusted for inflation)	$ 2,000	
Moonlighting	—	$ 5,000

Assets

Certificates of Deposit	$ 20,000	
IRA	$ 16,000	$ 16,000
Principal residence equity	$180,000	$125,000
Savings account	—	—

(This is an approximate estimate. The Wilsons used their CD to get into their new home. They may have borrowed additional money as well.)

	Fast Track	Good Life
Debts		
Mortgage	$120,000	?
Future (college)		$25,000

If your current level of income is not as high as that of the Wilsons or if you are renting and do not own property, the following example may be more representative of your circumstances:

Christie Thomas is a single parent. She is an advertising accountant and has two young girls in parochial school. She earns $68,000. She rents an apartment in San Francisco. The following is her current expense budget:

	July	August	September
Clothing			
everyday:	$ 45	—	—
work clothes:	$ 35	$ 80	$ 130
schoolclothes:	—	$ 140	$ 75
extras:	$ 15	—	—
Credit cards			
total monthly payments:	$ 220	$ 220	$ 220
Education			
monthly tuition:	$ 300	$ 300	$ 300
school supplies:	—	—	$ 95
lessons:	—	—	$ 15
Entertainment			
dinners, parties:	—	—	—
movies:	$ 50	$ 50	$ 50
video rentals:	$ 10	$ 5	—
miscellaneous:	$ 15	$ 15	—
books, magazines:	$ 20	$ 20	$ 20

	July	August	September
Food			
groceries:	$ 180	$ 180	$ 180
eating out:	$ 65	$ 130	—
Gifts	$ 25	$ 15	$ 20
Housing			
monthly rental:	$ 975	$ 975	$ 975
property tax:	—	—	—
home repairs:	—	—	—
home supplies:	—	—	$ 35
Insurance			
health:	employer paid		
disability & life:	$ 100	$ 100	$ 100
house:	—	—	—
car:	$ 75	$ 75	$ 75
Medical (covered)			
unexpected:	$ 150	—	—
Miscellaneous			
pets:	$ 15	$ 15	$ 15
church, charity:	$ 25	$ 25	$ 25
Phone	$ 50	$ 45	$ 60
Taxes (monthly)			
federal & state:	$1150	$1150	$1150
Transportation (1 car)			
gas:	$ 65	$ 55	$ 70
carwash:	$ 5	$ 5	$ 5
car payment:	$ 155	$ 155	$ 155
maintenance:	—	—	—
miscellaneous:	$ 145 (registration)	—	—

	July	August	September
Utilities			
oil/gas:	$ 10	$ 10	$ 10
electric:	$ 20	$ 20	$ 20
water:	$ 10	$ 10	$ 10
Totals:	$3930	$3795	$3810

Christie's average monthly overhead is $3845. She plans to move to a small town in Georgia where she will teach in the community college. Her future income will be $32,000. She has already begun looking into the cost of living in the town she plans to move to and has been estimating her future monthly expenses. She needs to know before she arrives exactly how much she will be able to spend on food, housing, and other essentials. Although she is uncertain what she will pay for taxes, she has estimated that her monthly living expenses cannot exceed $2,000 per month. This will give her a cushion of money to set aside for unexpected expenses in addition to the cost of moving when she relocates. She has prepared a tentative budget.

LIVING EXPENSES

(Average per 3 months)	Fast Track	Good Life
Clothing	$ 175	$ 100
Credit cards	$ 220	—
Education	$ 335	$ 200
Entertainment	$ 85	$ 40
Food	$ 245	$ 150
Gifts	$ 20	$ 10
Housing	$ 985	$ 450
Insurance	$ 175	$ 150
Medical	$ 50	$ 50
Miscellaneous	$ 40	$ 30
Phone	$ 50	$ 25
Tax	$ 1150	$ 500
Transportation	$ 815	$ 250
Utilities	$ 50	$ 50

Income (yearly)

| Salary | $68,000 | $32,000 |

(Average per 3 months)	*Fast Track*	*Good Life*
Interest Income		
(not adjusted for inflation)	—	—
Moonlighting	—	—
Assets		
Certificates of Deposit	—	—
IRA	—	—
Principal residence equity	—	—
Savings account	$ 7000	$ 7000
Debts		
Mortgage	—	—
Future (college)	$40,000	$40,000

Knowing in advance what your future income will be allows you to estimate what you can or cannot afford once you relocate. (This may also affect your choice of where you want to live.)

As you do your research into the new area, ask questions about the expenses you anticipate—utilities, car insurance, phone service, food, and so on. Try to get a picture of the general cost of living. Every time you learn the cost of something in the new area, write it down on your Expenses Estimate Chart in your journal.

> We rent the downstairs of a beautiful Victorian house for $320 a month. But we weren't expecting the oil bill for last January to be $220!
>
> DIANE SANDERS
> *Northern Michigan*

> When we arrived in Jonesboro, Arkansas, we were delighted to find that everything—especially housing—was so less expensive than what we were accustomed to paying in Houston. We were on a budget in Houston, and it was like somebody released the pressure valve.
>
> ALLISON PETERS

SAVE NOW, AND SPEND WISELY. Saving now while you are still earning fast money is the smartest, most pragmatic tactic you can make before your move. Chances are you will probably never earn the kind of money you are earning now once you step off the fast track. The majority of ex-FTers had saved enough money to last them a year before they made the move.

> If you pay cash for everything, it'll crimp your style right away. I'd recommend paying cash for everything outside of business expenses those first two years (off the fast track). It's the perfect incentive to hang on to your money.
>
> PETER KIRSCH
> *Rhinelander, Wisconsin*

Learn to distinguish between the necessary and the superfluous, between what you can use and what will be wasted. A stoic commitment to changing your habits is necessary. Look at saving money not as a deprivation but as a positive step toward living the good life.

Not spending money can become habit-forming.

ANONYMOUS

Having to "use it up, wear it out, make it do or do without—our 11th commandment—has caused us to really think about what is important. Unlike some of our city friends, we have to be sure we really need it before making any major purchase. We have a lot less of the things that can be bought, but a lot more of the things that can't be. (*Countryside*, August, 1982)

> TRENA WALLACE
> *Magnolia, Kentucky*

An ancient Oriental saying reveals: "A man can measure his wealth by what he can do without." When you are considering any purchase, ask yourself:

- Is there a way of meeting the need without buying something?

- Is it essential? Can I live without it?

- Can it wait until next month? When the next month rolls around, ask yourself the same question: Can it wait until next month? If it can't, then you probably need it. If you wait long enough, you may be able to get it on sale or buy an improved product.

- Why exactly do you want it? Does it fit within the context of your vision of the good life?

- If it's a service, can you have it done for less, or can you do it yourself?

Purchase *now* what you will need later. It is a lot less painful to buy what you'll need to set up housekeeping and business now when you are making a lot of money than to wait until your finances are fixed and somewhat frozen. It can be a genuine shocker to go from earning $100,000 a year to earning $25,000 a year. Buying what you will need now instead of later (for example, office equipment, tools, inventory) will also force you to tighten your budget and spend money more wisely in advance of your move.

You must also begin setting money aside toward financing the research into the area you are considering moving to. You will have extra phone bills, books and reference materials, travel, and the costs of spending a weekend in the new area and making a longer visit after that. Visiting the area may also mean an unpaid temporary leave of absence from work, which *you* will have to compensate for.

You must also prepare for the cost of the move itself. If you have been hired by a new employer or are being transferred to a new office, ask if your employer can help pay for the cost of the move. Otherwise, call local or national moving companies for competitive estimates. Give them the mileage and a good description of what you own that will be shipped. This is an expense many don't anticipate, and it can be a whopper if you have a house full of furniture. Anticipate a week or more to do the moving. Figure the cost of lodging and meals if you are traveling some distance across the country. Plan a minibudget specifically related to expenses you will incur in making the move, and begin now to save for it.

> To accustom one's self, therefore, to simple and inexpensive habits is a great ingredient in the perfecting of health, and makes a man free from hesitation with respect to the necessary uses of life.
>
> EPICURUS

CONSULT A FINANCIAL ADVISOR. You may need a good tax person if you are liquidating assets, especially if you are selling collectibles or an equity-rich principal residence. You will face the prospect of paying high capital gains tax (unless you decide to lease your principal residence until you sell after age 55 and receive up to $125,000 in tax-free capital appreciation). Most need the money from the sale of their homes, however.

Because the financial needs of most ex-FTers are specific to their particular circumstances, I recommend you seek the advice of at least one professional who understands the goals you have set up for yourself. Find a financial advisor with whom you feel comfortable (you may have to interview a few before you find one you like), and let him or her analyze your current situation and make recommendations regarding your future circumstances. Your journal will come in handy for providing necessary details. You might consider talking with financial planners both in your current location and in the place you plan to move to.

Resources

Consult your phone book yellow pages under "Financial Planners," "CFA—Certified Financial Planner," "Tax and Financial Services," or "Accountants."

Contact: Institute for Certified Financial Planners
10065 E. Harvard Ave., Suite 320
Denver, CO 80231

The Licensed Independent Network of CPA Financial Planners
404 James Robertson Parkway, Suite 100
Nashville, TN 37219

International Association for Financial Planning
2 Converse Parkway, Suite 800
Atlanta, GA 30328

National Association of Personal Financial Advisors
P.O. Box 2026
Arlington Heights, IL 60006

Fail-Safe Options

Having savings invested to generate interest income is one "fail-safe" plan to consider. If you sold your home and have decided to rent after relocating instead of buying a residence, you can invest the equity you pulled from the sale of your principal residence. Many fast-trackers, however, currently rent or lease. If you are one of them, consider renting or leasing a less expensive residence and dramatically cutting back your living expenses before you make your move to get out, so you can immediately begin to set money aside for future interest income.

In his book *Cashing In on the American Dream*, Paul Terhorst advises selling your home, renting, and investing the money (after paying capital gains) in "safe, high-yield, trouble-free CDs that throw off enough cash to live on." Much of Terhorst's "American Dream" hinges on *not* owning a house after leaving the fast track in order to keep your overhead down. For many ex-FTers, however, owning a house with a backyard is part of their idea of living the good life.

Another option is to lease (or sublease) your apartment, town-house, condominium, or other principal residence, using that monthly income to help pay living expenses once you get off the fast track (this means you would rent in the new location, provided that this would be more economical than buying a primary residence).

> You might consider leasing your principal residence until you are 55; then sell it and receive as much as $125,000 in tax-free capital appreciation. While you lease, repairs and upkeep are tax-deductible.
>
> GAETON RIOPEL
> *Realtor*

The very best fail-safe plan you can have is a second means of earning income. You can do this by developing a second business that is different from your regular work, by taking on temporary jobs, or by doing part-time work. You can moonlight (doing any of the above three options) while you are still on the fast track in order to put aside extra money for your future move. You can also moonlight once you have relocated as a way of earning extra income in case you are waiting for a job opening or for your business to grow, or simply as a way to supplement whatever income you will be earning.

One more consideration that may or may not be considered fail-safe but is crucial in your long-term financial plan is the necessity of keeping up with inflation by setting aside an additional 5% annually (more if you can afford it) into your regular savings.

If, despite all precautions, you do find yourself in trouble financially, the solution—odd as it may seem—is to relax. Don't panic. You can always find some temporary job to hold you over, even if it's washing dishes. Every great entrepreneur will tell you that there isn't a single job from which you can't learn something that will help you in your future endeavors.

DECIDING ON A TRANSITION STRATEGY

Some ex-FTers take six months to make the transition, and others take ten years. Some do it when their children are young; others wait until their children graduate from high school. Some wait for more financial security before they make the move, while some leave when their finances are in jeopardy.

> It took us about six months to make the move to Lake Havasu, Arizona. We left the city all but broke. When we arrived here, we rented and we worked and we worked and we worked. I'd say we jumped from the hot pan into the fire. But today we have a thriving business shipping our model airplanes all over the world.
>
> BOB AND KATIE MARTIN
> Entrepreneurs
> Lake Havasu, Arizona

Test the Water: A Foot in Both Worlds

If your circumstances prevent you from making a quick transition or if you feel uncertain about the move, there are ways of drawing out the transition period and keeping the door open if you decide to change your mind.

BUY OR RENT A SECOND HOME.   If the long-range goals you developed in chapter 3 require you to stay on the fast track a few more years, you might consider buying an affordable second (vacation) home in the area you think you might want to move to. It is an excellent way to slowly become acquainted with the community. If you are in a high tax bracket, there is the added bonus of having the mortgage interest deduction. If possible, pay off as much of the house as you can while you're still on the fast track. This is not contrary to your "tightening-the-belt budget" since it can be an important step toward realizing your goals. In fact, having the extra financial burden of the second home may force you onto a budget and help to cut unnecessary expenditures. The second home, meanwhile, should appreciate in value with inflation.

Robin and Peter Moyer were not intending to get off the fast track when they purchased their vacation home in Jackson, Wyoming. But after they became familiar with the community and the area, and learned that it was possible for them to find work locally, they used it as the stepping-stone to permanent residency.

Kirstie Wilde and her husband Paul Miller bought a small vacation house in Pacific Grove, California. Within a few years they became full-time residents, working as TV anchor and news director for a local television station. After becoming permanent residents, they sold their first house and bought oceanside acreage. They fell in love with the clean air, the sea breezes, and the small-town ambience in which to raise their children.

Some make the transition from spending weekends at their second home in the country to permanent residence over a period of several years.

> The Parkers had spent weekends in this area for more than ten years before they decided to become permanent residents. Mr. Parker, who owned a wholesale antiques business in Queens, spent part of that time buying and restoring an unused church in Spencertown. Shortly after the family moved here to stay, he opened an art and antiques shop in the former church. (*New York Times*, December 31, 1987)

COMMUTING.   Tom and Pat Garbrecht purchased Stonehouse, their bed-and-breakfast in St. Germaine, Wisconsin, before they were ready to start up the business. Pat moved into the house full time to begin renovation, while Tom commuted between Ohio and northern Wisconsin whenever he could get free time from his job as a chemist—one or two weekends a month and all of his vacation time. After a year of preparation, Tom left his job in Ohio, and they were ready to open for business.

Gary Regester and his wife Joanie (see chapter 4) commuted between Los Angeles and Silver Plume, Colorado, for two years before completing the transition.

Moving—with Caution

You've found a place where you think you'd like to live and work. You've done a little homework investigating the area. You've visited for a weekend. Meanwhile, at the home front, you have a payment schedule set up to start paying off the credit cards, and you have saved some money.

You've decided to spend two weeks checking out work opportunities and real estate in the new area. While there, you happen upon the house of your dreams. You want to put money down immediately. Stop! The biggest mistakes are made at this stage of the quest. The following paragraphs can help you avoid some common pitfalls.

GO SLOWLY.   Individuals may be coming from relatively lavish backgrounds, and they believe that getting a home that simply costs less than the one they now have is all that matters. They believe paying cash for the house and eliminating mortgage payments gives them the green light on "happily ever after." Too many failed ex-Fters can attest to the naïveté of such rash investments.

While the cost of living may be far less in the new location, bear in mind that wages and salaries in the area will also be less—so go slowly.

> What we both weren't quite expecting was the difference in pay scale. . . . An engineer with my kind of experience can only earn half of what I made in Irvine [CA]. Pay scales are abominable. . . . I called up the owner of a company that manufactures equipment for the apple orchards. He said, "Oh yes, we hire engineers. Harry just retired in 1984. I think the next guy is going to retire in 1992—call me then!" People get on waiting lists for jobs for two years! They get one half of a real paycheck and they are so happy to get the job they stay with it until they are ready to retire!
>
> DOM SMELLER
> Wenatchee, Washington

A second common mistake is to overestimate the profit you will earn from the sale of your house. Some realize too late that they do not have the extra capital they thought they would have to invest in a new business—a business they were counting on for income.

A third common mistake is to reinvest all of the profit from the sale of the principal residence into a more expensive house in order to avoid paying capital gains. You find yourself in the same boat overwhelmed by debt, shouldering the burden of another high mortgage payment. You also risk ending up with a white elephant, costly to maintain and difficult to sell in a sluggish real estate market.

> Because of stagnant housing markets in other parts of the country, a comfortable, affordable well-built house on a friendly tree-lined street can go begging for a buyer for as long as a year. People who

leave New York and Los Angeles for quieter, less frenetic places sometimes find that the way out of town is a one-way street. In the time they were gone, prices have gone up so fast they now can't qualify to buy the house they once lived in. (*Los Angeles Times*, March 3, 1989)

If you can, you want to invest straight across so you don't have to pay taxes on your capital gains. On the other hand, we have professionals—a lot of stockbrokers—who want to invest a chunk of money in a new business here. I'd say you'd want to come in with at least $100,000 to invest in a small business—that's in addition to what you'll need for living expenses and buying a home. If you rent for a while you keep your capital intact and can live off the interest. A lot of small businesses won't take contingencies and so I believe there is a fair degree of risk. Those boys with the BMA are more likely to figure it out. Most of them will be working just as hard as before but without the same debt threshold—that is an automatic improvement in the quality of life.

PETER PARNEGG
Albuquerque, New Mexico

The most cautious way to move is to rent or lease, with your capital temporarily earning you interest, until you have become well acclimated in the new community and in your new work.

Don't let your excitement about your new life cause you to rush in hastily. There will be plenty of time to look around and find the home of your dreams. You want to be certain that this new place is the right choice for you and your family.

Once we started thinking about leaving L.A., it was six months later that we moved. We considered and looked into three other areas of the country. When we arrived in Minneapolis, we rented for three months before buying a house. I had a six-month contract with my illustrators in L.A., so that helped me make the transition. It took two months to get acclimated here. Before coming here I laid groundwork making lists of all the agencies and art directors. I was also lucky to have the best photographer in the city call to ask me to represent him. . . . I spend mornings on appointments and have the rest of the day to spend with my family.

ROBIN OGDEN
Minneapolis, Minnesota

If you decide to buy instead of rent, consider creative options not suggested by many brokers and banks:

- Try a lease-option. The contract can be written to give the buyer as much time as needed to purchase the house with a portion of the monthly lease going toward final purchase price—an excellent alternative to renting.

- Look for a pre-foreclosure. By assuming an owner's delinquent mortgage payments, a house in pre-foreclosure can be obtained provided the current owners are open to negotiating for a small cash down. You can find out about pre-foreclosures from the owners themselves, a local realtor, or the talk around town.

- Check county courthouse records for probate or estate sales.

- Ask the seller to finance the deal.

- Consider a land contract—many resort properties can be purchased on a contingency basis.

- Buy repossessed properties. To do this you can meet with the real estate officers at the local banks and S&Ls. Ask what is available on their REOs (Real Estate Owned) list or ask them to call when something comes in.

A small percentage of ex-FTers relocate a second time after finding they are dissatisfied with their first choice. The reasons given for their dissatisfaction are reasons that usually could have been foreseen: misplaced priorities, inadequate research, unrealistic expectations, and so on. Scott McLaughlin is a good example. He was eager to leave New York City, where he had been working in the advertising industry. Because his work primarily involved telecommunications, he could live practically anywhere in the country. He chose to move to Bloomington, Indiana, to be near family. He underestimated, however, how much he depended on his active social life and how much he wanted to ski all winter. After two years of growing frustration, he decided to move to Denver, Colorado. Denver suits him perfectly, and he is content visiting his family on holidays and vacations.

Act quickly, think slowly.

GREEK PROVERB

You may discover that despite all of your research and predictions, you can't earn enough money to survive. Or perhaps the community is different from what you expected. Perhaps you've found out that there is a toxic waste dump nearby. Reasons to move to another location usually surface in the first year of residency—so, *wait on the purchase of property.* The government gives you two years before you have to reinvest the profit from the sale of your former principal residence before it taxes you on the capital gains.

MOONLIGHTING.   Moonlighting means holding a second job in addition to a regular one. Some successful ex-FTers used second jobs to earn extra money to help them get started in their new careers. Others work second jobs to earn extra money once they step off the fast track. After quitting his fast track career as a systems analyst, Mike Powers worked both as a dairy farmer and as an auto parts salesman.

Linda Evangelist is eager to leave Chicago where she works as an art teacher at a gifted children's secondary school. She would like to move to a smaller city in South Carolina near where she grew up, but is concerned she will not be able to earn enough money as a part-time teacher (she knows it will be difficult finding full-time employment as an art teacher). During her free time, Friday afternoons and weekends, she works with private clients as an art therapist. She became qualified to do this during the past two years and believes that moonlighting as an art therapist will make it financially feasible to relocate to a smaller community.

Developing a business on the side while continuing to work a regular job is a cautious, less risky way of beginning the transition off the fast track. While working for IBM, Anthony Temesch purchased modestly priced resort property to manage. He now manages those properties full time. Now, after quitting his job, Pete Polsen, a physicist, began putting his own business together while working for defense contractors in the city. He now operates his own business solving sensor problems out of his home in Grants Pass, Oregon.

Several successful ex-FTers developed skills and contacts before leaving their fast-track careers that have enabled them to moonlight doing consulting and other part-time business work to earn supplementary income.

Charles Fuller is an example of someone who learned a craft while continuing to work his regular job. Fuller was a mechanical maintenance supervisor at a nuclear power plant in Florida. He and his family used to drive up to Tennessee to enjoy the country. In 1974, he came across an ad in *Mother Earth News* for a blacksmithing school in Lebanon, New Hampshire. He enrolled in the course, which took four weeks to complete. Within a month he saw a want ad in a Tennessee newspaper seeking a blacksmith to work at a theme park. He got the job and relocated to Tennessee, moving his family to a cottage in a beautiful valley outside Pigeon Forge. "It was nothing like the fancy house we'd had in Florida . . . but it became home. I could garden, and the valley took my breath away" (*Mother Earth News*, March, 1988). He worked at the job until 1984, when he opened his own business, The Broken Anvil, in Pigeon Forge.

PREPARING PSYCHOLOGICALLY FOR THE MOVE

Plan to do a few of the activities now that you will be doing once you move. If you are planning to move to an area where you will be hiking in the country, take a weekend off now to give your family a feeling of what's to come.

If you plan to switch careers entirely, try to get a feeling for what it will be like not to be working the same job anymore. Most people are so accustomed to working all of the time that when they receive unscheduled free time they are at a loss how to spend it. Take a few days off from work and do something that is out of the ordinary for you. It will feel strange, and you may have an uncomfortable feeling of guilt that you should be working! Look around and see how many others are taking in an early matinee, lounging at the library, taking the kids to the zoo. There are people like you at the hardware store, at the plaza, at the post office—running errands or enjoying time off. You need to get a feeling for what it will be like not to punch the time clock. Your psyche may be so attuned to your work that it may be a real shocker emotionally to be suddenly without it.

Set a Departure Date

Give yourself a time limit—three months, six months, two years. Keep in mind the old axiom that one gets done what needs to get done in the exact amount of time available. Visualize the move. See it in your mind. Try to imagine what it will be like, based on your research and experience. If you have difficulty here, it may be because you haven't enough material to go on—you are not familiar enough with the new environment, the people, the work. Make a list of all the things you are looking forward to doing once you have made the move off the fast track. Your spouse and children should make up their own lists or be reminded of the interests they will have in the new area. Keep the family in anticipation of the move rather than dwelling on what they will leave behind. Remind yourself and your family that friends and family will visit and stay in touch after the move.

No one knows better than you when you should make your move. Much depends on your plan. You've done the "pregame warm-up," laid the groundwork in the new location for both work and family needs, and kept your objectives in order.

When you make your move, you should feel both confident and comfortable with your decision. Every detail—large and small—should have been attended to. Is the new house or apartment ready for you? Granted, there are those who are so bold as to arrive without a place to stay, but this is hardly recommended! Have all loose ends been tied up for the residence you are leaving behind? Have medical and school records been transferred? Have local accounts been settled and closed? Have you notified the post office (and all pertinent business contacts) of your new address? Do the neighbors have your new phone number and address in case they need to get in touch with you? Well in advance of the move, make a checklist with your spouse and family members of all the details to take care of. Jot this list down in your journal, and check it off as each item is done.

Have a Fallback Plan

What will you do if things don't work out? How long should you give it before throwing in the towel?

First, give all that you have to give so you won't be questioning yourself 20 years from now! If your problem is specific to the location, you can pursue one of the two backup location options you selected in chapter 4. However, before you move to the next location, do some troubleshooting to make sure that what went wrong in the first place won't go wrong in the second.

If your troubles are bigger than your choice of place—if what you have discovered is that you don't like being off the fast track—then you can use this experience to return to something better. No one regrets having taken the chance to get out, because the adventure has made them wiser, stronger, and more confident.

Once you have a plan of action and a financial strategy in place, follow to the best of your ability the timeframe you have set for both your short-term and long-term goals. Any questions, ideas, objections, or problems that surface as you prepare to step off the fast track and into your new life should be written down in your journal. Changing circumstances or a previously unforeseen opportunity may require some last-minute adjusting of your gameplan. Keep an open mind. Enjoy the process.

SUGGESTED READING

ELGIN, DUANE, and MITCHELL, ARNOLD. "Voluntary Simplicity: Life-Style of the Future." *Futurist* 11 (1977):200–209.

LONG, CHARLES. *How to Survive Without a Salary.* Toronto: Summerhill Press, 1988.

SCHER, LES. *Finding and Buying Your Place in the Country.* New York: Collier Books, 1974.

SCHUMACHER, E. F. *Small Is Beautiful.* New York: Harper & Row, 1973.

TAUBER, EDWARD. *How to Retire Young.* Homewood, Ill.: Dow Jones-Irwin, 1989.

TERHORST, PAUL. *Cashing In on the American Dream.* New York: Bantam Books, 1988.

6

The test of any man lies in action.

PINDAR

Making Your Move

BUSINESS MANAGER TURNED MEDICAL TECHNICIAN

Ellen Kimble worked as a business manager and accountant for an illustration and photography studio in Burbank, California, for 20 years. She is originally from Marfa, Texas, where she worked as an R.N. During time spent in California, she did volunteer work at the children's hospital. Since returning to Texas, she has received additional medical training.

> The city drove me batty. It smells funny, it's dirty, crowded, it's not safe. The city is no place to raise your teenager.
> Since moving here, I spend a lot of time in the country doing mountain climbing, hiking, and gathering up a lot of rocks and cattle skulls to make art work—the ultimate in recycling!
> Marfa has a population of 2,000 and stretches across five miles from one city sign to the other. The last commercial business closes at 10 P.M. around here. That means no restaurants, no gas stations, nothing is open after 10.

Here you don't have that dog-eat-dog, scrambling-to-the-top attitude you find in the city. Maybe because here it's economically depressed across the board. Everybody feels it. Even the wealthy have been hit pretty hard here. Then we have the miserably poor. Per capita, I believe they are poorer than the Appalachians.

When I first got here, I took a job earning $5 an hour. I supported a teenage son on a gross pay of $5 an hour! And we've had a wonderful time! There's nothing we're sorry about not having. No one else has anything either so it doesn't bother you. If I wanted to, I could go into any store in town and sign my name and get whatever I want on credit and pay for it when I have the money. There's nothing we are really wanting for, though at times it has gotten pretty lean.

My leisure time is drastically different. We take off for excursions down into Mexico and then about 45 miles from here is Big Ben National Park, one of the most beautiful national parks in the United States. It is magnificent country. Legend has it that when God finished making the earth, he had a bunch of stuff left over and dumped it all in a big pile and called it Big Ben. They have something of everything there. When I used to fly my Cessna out of Burbank Airport I would call in and if visibility was four and a half miles that was incredible. Here, from Big Ben, visibility is 200 miles! It took a while to get used to such clear, clean air.

Since moving here, there has been a 180-degree change in my son. Back in the city, he used to come up with every excuse in the world why he didn't want to go to school or wouldn't do his homework. Now he is a straight-A student. He is a leader instead of a mouse. He's tutoring younger kids in math. He won first place the last two years in the University Interscholastic League district competition for science. They were able to solicit a lot of support from the community—materials from the local lumberyard, financial support from the electrical company, a little old lady's fallout shelter for doing the photography because it was pitch black, carpentry skills from some—they even had faculty from the University at Alpine come down and critique their work!

The schools here don't have the advanced expensive things you have in the city schools, but they have something more important. They have teachers who are teaching because they love to teach and they love where they live. The science teacher drives 100 miles every day to teach at the junior high.

Kids here can find out who they are—doing all the crazy things kids do—and it's safe. If you get into trouble here you can get back out of trouble. In the city, if you get into trouble you are probably over your head. It's bigger than you.

Because of my job I am a very visible person. One doctor and I pretty much make up the whole medical staff. I'm on call 24 hours a day. I know everybody in town. I've become part of a very close-knit group. If you are an outsider coming into town, you need to come in knowing who you are and willing to share who you are with everyone.

I'd have to say that I have done more, learned more, and improved myself more in the last 18 months than I have in my whole life.

I think that in my heart I always knew I belonged here. I was in the city for more than 20 years, but I never really felt a part of it. I love this country. I love the sky. I love the dirt. And it loves me back.

ELLEN KIMBLE
Medical Staffer
Marfa, Texas

ENGINEER TURNED ELECTRICIAN

Don and Sandy Smeller and their two sons left Southern California and moved to central Washington on a fluke. Don remembers wanting to escape the city for a few days and visit Lake Chelan, near Wenatchee, Washington. While they were packing, a real estate agent called out of the blue and asked if they wanted to sell their house. Within two weeks, the Smellers had sold their house (for $207,000) and bought a new house in Wenatchee for ($157,000), on a hillside overlooking the Columbia River, the mountains, and endless apple orchards. Don started a new business working out of their home. Three years later, he whistles his amazement at the string of miracles that made it all happen.

The Smellers are examples of ex-FTers who left the fast track on an impulse, with little preparation. Although they faced a number of setbacks, they continued to "roll with the punches" and adapt to new opportunities. Their story demonstrates how perseverance, and the simple desire to make it work, can pull you through the most difficult of times.

We had gotten caught up in a "nuthouse" mentality, running from PTA to Little League to church functions to club activities. We didn't know if we were coming or going. Everyone we knew, including ourselves, seemed to be mortgaged to the hilt, husband and wife both working, fighting freeways, wondering how come the kids were running amok. At night you couldn't sleep because of the noise from the 405 and the 55, the John Wayne Airport, the Tustin U.S. Marine Corps Helicopter Station, and two six-lane boulevards. You couldn't open a window to let a little night breeze in.

We've been up here about three years now. It was sort of miraculous the way it happened. We had been vacationing up here for several years—my wife's sister lives here in Wenatchee. We'd come for one or two weeks, spending time at Lake Chelan, a beautiful, glacier-fed lake. My wife and her sister were kind of lonely for each other, and one day at home in Irvine we just started thinking how wonderful it would be if someday we could move up here. We were packing the motor home to come up over the Fourth of July when a strange thing happened. Our phone rang, and it was a real estate agent calling to say she had a buyer for our house— even though we hadn't put our house on the market!

Since we had just finished talking about wanting to move to Wenatchee, we said it was okay for them to come by. Well, the agent brought the buyers over and within 24 hours we had an offer on our home.

By sheer coincidence, my wife had written to a real estate agent in Wenatchee about a week before the sale of our house and had given her some specs on what we would like. She sent us back a number of possibilities. She had really done her homework.

We have two boys—they were 12 and 8 at the time—and they just fell in love with one of the houses. A friend of my sister-in-law happened to be the owner of the house! My wife went directly over to see the house—and, well, we bought it! All this had happened, and I still had no way of making a living up there.

But then a third in a series of miracles took place. My former employer called to ask if I was interested in starting up a small manufacturing operation. I had quit the company, Rainbird, in 1986 to do my own consulting work as an engineer. I said that I was planning to move to Washington, and he said that was okay— that I should just come in and meet with him and we could see if it was feasible.

This house we bought up here just happened to have an annex to it that made the perfect room for the manufacturing operation. I only had to walk 40 feet to go to work in the morning! The business was virtually self-contained. Rainbird sent me the parts, and I assembled them and put them on a truck for shipment. UPS, or another trucking outfit, picked them up right from my door. I did this for a year before both Rainbird and I decided I couldn't make a living—there wasn't enough volume. It just wasn't working out. We were supplementing our income with savings to get by, and they were being depleted.

About this time, my wife started casting about for a job, and she landed a great one as personnel manager for a food-processing plant nearby. Recently, though, they moved 38 miles away, so my wife is back to being a commuter.

For six months I looked for a job, with only a couple of short-term projects in between for draftsman's pay. There are absolutely no professional jobs advertised in the newspaper, but you can get a job at MacDonald's. I learned very quickly that to find any other sort of job, you have to know somebody.

Before college I had learned the electrician trade—my father was in the business. So I called a friend and told him about my experience as an electrician, and in a month I had a job as one. I went in at age 43 as a highly overqualified apprentice. This brings up one of the major frustrations I've run into: you work for people who may not know as much as you, and it is extremely difficult to suggest to your boss that there is a better way to do a certain job. They don't want to hear it. And it can be so incredibly frustrating to stand by and do something that you know isn't being done properly or with any regard to quality. Especially coming from where I did, being in charge of big budgets, people, and the re-sources to do a good job.

Then I got laid off. That's the lifestyle of tradesmen here in East Washington—seasonal work and getting laid off. Those with a journeyman's card are the only ones to survive the winter here—they have gone through a four-year apprentice program, taken a test, and gotten their cards. But the apprentices all get laid off. Quite a few head for Seattle, which is what I did. I worked in Seattle, lived in my mobile home there, and came home for weekends. But for what I made after the expenses of renting a place for the mobile home, driving back and forth all that time, I might as well have been flipping hamburgers at McDonalds! Plus, I really missed my family.

Right now I have an invention I've been working on that I want to get patented. The money I paid in taxes when I left Irvine was what I was hoping to invest in this invention. Now I have to find another source of capital—and I have time to do it, with the layoff situation.

One major drawback to moving here was the IRS ramifica-tions—capital gains, for instance. The government wants you to buy a house of equal or greater value than the house you are selling. If you don't, you just end up paying that money to the government. We were trying to escape the insanity of high mortgages—all of our friends in California are mortgaged out and have to work and work and work in order to pay them. But when you move to a location like this, you have a real cash strain after paying 28% of what you thought you had in profit to the government. We sold our Xerox copy business to the real estate woman who had helped us, and the government was right there to take our money. If you can't pay it right away, you are slapped with some pretty stiff penalties. My advice to anyone planning to get out is to hire a very good tax specialist. Let him map out the realities. Seeing it coming doesn't blunt it, but at least it prevents you from making any stupid blind decisions.

We joined the Presbyterian church here, but as far as being social, we've held ourselves back. We have plenty of things to do, and we have rethought the calendar. We choose not to do so many things. Also, here it is sort of cliqueish. There is an inner circle, and we are the outsiders looking in. Being from California is not an asset. People snicker when they hear you are from California. California jokes are like ethnic jokes. But, you know, if your inner security depends on a circle of friends, then you are probably going to be unhappy.

We have a great house, we have the kids' college education all set, and we have a motor home. The kids are having fun, we've got a highly rated school system, my wife has a job she loves and finds challenging, and me—I have time to stop and think. And I haven't had a single headache since we moved here!

Don and Sandy Smeller
Tradesman and Manager
Wenatchee, Washington

LEAVING THE FAST TRACK BEHIND

The day has come to make your move. Not unlike other ex-FTers, you are probably feeling a little frightened. A healthy dose of the heebie-jeebies is natural and to be expected. You have come a long way, as far back as that first glimmer in your imagination that life could be simpler and more fulfilling. After months of preparation and difficult decisions affecting your career, your family, your finances, and so on, you are ready to take the final step. It is the easiest, simplest step of the journey. You have already laid the groundwork. Having purpose and direction in your life gives you the staying power and the conviction that will finally take you home.

The day we packed up to head out, I had a sudden feeling of foreboding that I mentioned to Steve. He thought it was funny and told me to relax. Then he made a joke and said we probably wouldn't survive the traffic out of the city anyway! I felt like I was giving up security—our jobs, our friends, our home. As soon as we entered the freeway heading West, I had an incredible surge of energy and excitement. Steve felt it, too. You feel separate and apart from everybody else, as if you have broken free and the sky is the limit.

Our doubts are traitors / And make us lose the good we oft might win / By fearing to attempt.

SHAKESPEARE
Measure for Measure

When you have an objective worth risking for, your actions become purposeful and your life begins to make sense, and then no risk can hold you back.

DAVID VISCOTT

PAIGE AND STEVE LAWRENCE
Bozeman, Montana

We were nervous, but that passed as soon as we got going. Right away, we started looking forward to a list of things we had been planning to do. Karen had a notebook and was making a list of all the things she wanted to do after we got unpacked and settled. The first thing she said she wanted to do was take a stroll around the neighborhood as the sun was coming up. And she did!

KAREN AND TED HEMINGWAY
Cedar Rapids, Iowa

I was sad about leaving behind what had been home for over 10 years. I thought about all of the hours of hard work it had taken to make it a home, all of the great memories . . . and yet what I kept trying to remember was that we wanted a home where our children, and someday maybe our grandchildren, would happily come back to visit. We were looking for a sense of tradition that neither of us had in our own families—you know, the house-in-the-country-four-generations-later kind of thing. We didn't think that would be possible in the city—where there were too many changes going on around us that were out of our control.

TYRIE AND ANDREW DAWSON
Charlottesville, Virginia

If you find yourself postponing the departure date, there may be a monkey wrench in the works. Find out what precisely is holding you up. There are many factors at work having to do with your family and friends, your finances, your job, your home. As you make the transition off the fast track, these various elements must all be synchronized with one another. If one element is neglected or ignored, it will affect all of the others.

Are any of the following questions unanswered?

1. Have you arranged for work in the new location, and are you prepared to begin working soon after your arrival?

2. Do you have enough money to survive for at least one year?

3. Have you rented a place to stay? Is it ready for you?

4. Have you made contacts in the new location whom you can ask for help if you need it?

5. Has every family member at least one personal interest to look forward to?

6. Have you completed the list in your journal of all the things to do before leaving?

7. Are your finances in order? (Have you received financial counseling? Are your credit cards paid off? Have you resolved all financial matters having to do with the sale of any property?)

If you can honestly answer yes to all of the questions above but are still having difficulty leaving, postpone your departure, give yourself a few more days, perhaps a week, to relax and review the choices you have made thus far. Give careful thought to what you have written in your journal. Sooner or later, whatever is bothering you will surface and you will be able to confront it head-on.

MOVING IN: WHAT TO EXPECT

The likelihood that the locals will be as excited as you are about your arrival is slim. No one may even notice! Many successful ex-FTers agree that you have to take the initiative and make things happen if you are looking to become involved in the life of your new community. This is especially true if you are operating your own business and depend on local patronage.

Anthony Stevens was a banker for Citicorp in Washington, D.C., before he left the fast track to become an organic farmer in West Virginia. He wasted no time making contacts in the new area, and he joined a regional farmers' cooperative. That organization made it possible for him to meet other farmers and to learn more about growing produce through their practical advice. According to an article in *Countryside* magazine (Winter, 1990), "The co-op also buys [Stevens's] produce and has been crucial to sustaining the farm financially."

The experiences of several other ex-FTers mentioned in earlier chapters demonstrate the wisdom of volunteering for or participating in local organizations. Christmas-tree farmer Bruce Niedermeier is one example:

> I became a volunteer for the tree association and editor for the newspaper. It was a great way to learn a lot fast. . . . We have a nonprofit organization called the Wisconsin Christmas Tree Producers Association. . . . Their publication used to be a 6-page mimeographed sheet and now we have a 32-page glossy. . . . In three years I got to know everybody. . . . We have a direct-mail campaign, a buyer's guide, retailer tips. . . . I do all the market research for free. . . . We have a complete data base of potential buyers. All of this has meant that I've learned a lot about every facet of the business. I am a strong believer that if you give something you get back a whole lot more. Because of my volunteer work for the association I have vastly improved my writing skills, and because of my honest approach, I have built a lot of trust with all the people I work with.

Adjusting Socially

For some people, making new friends and attempting to "fit in" becomes the biggest obstacle to overcome once they have relocated. Others never give it a second thought. The advice from most ex-FTers is to take your time and not rush things (contrary to the advice mentioned above for making work-related contracts).

If you run into a few people who resent outsiders, try to empathize. The following excerpt from a letter written to the *Los Angeles Times* from a resident of a small city in Oregon captures one local point of view.

> I think it should be a rule for persons coming to a new country, always first to follow the customs of that country as closely as possible, reserving their improvements till they get firmly established, and see good reason to apply them.
>
> CAPTAIN BASIL HALL
> *Travels in North America*

Housing prices have always been in accordance with our local economy. Almost all jobs are service jobs. Any hourly wage over $6 is considered good, and yet, until recently, with some sacrifice, locals might have a chance of buying a home. Unfortunately, that situation has changed in the last year or so. Migrants from your area have quickly driven housing prices beyond the means of most locals, and rent prices have followed as well. Residents here have a fierce loyalty to the area, and yet are beginning to feel squeezed out, all for the benefit of people from outside the area and real estate agents. So when your readers show up here with wads of cash in their pockets and don't see the smiles they expected, I'm hoping they will have some perspective on where the resentment is coming from.

Robert Johnson
Bend, Oregon

Many advise that you refrain from giving advice to locals about their community until you have really become a part of the community.

The trick to a happy move is biding your time, neither flaunting your differences nor trying too hard to mimic local manners and ways. Use that time to survey the local society, see how it works, and then decide just where you would fit in.

Charles Long
Life after the City

Ask folks for advice, don't be givin' it.

Anonymous
Billings, Montana

Take confidence in your own resiliency. Some ex-FTers arrived a lot less prepared than you probably will be!

I arrived here not knowing a soul except for my boss. When I arrived at the airport, I bought my first map of the place. I didn't have an apartment, I didn't have a car. I stayed with my boss's family two weeks before I found a place. But what an adventure! I think everybody should do this at least once in their life. It makes you grow as a person. Just jump in with all fours. Everything will fall into place.

That I was working for the chamber of commerce made my involvement in the community a lot easier. Now I do a lot of volunteer work with Junior Achievement and United Way.

Jody Rush
Austin, Texas

A woman I know who moved here as a complete stranger managed in two years to meet and become friends with every mover and shaker in the city—and I mean the mayor, the state senator, and anyone who was what you'd call important. It took dedication, interest, and her people skills. She'd call them up and "do dinner." She had a contribution to make to the community, and she plugged herself right in. I believe this is true of most places in Middle America; it just takes initiative, and you can hang out with anybody you want to.

PETER PARNEGG
Albuquerque, New Mexico

Being the new kid on the block can be tough for children of any age. Some parents suggest that one of the best ways of making new friends in school and in the neighborhood is to invite kids over.

The three oldest kids in school—Allison in seventh grade, Cody in third grade, and Austen in kindergarten—invited someone over for after school, and for Saturday, and even for dinner that first week we were here. They made friends right away. I don't remember having any problems.

LESLEY KIRSCH
Stevenspoint, Wisconsin

Just be nice. If somebody else isn't nice, don't pay any attention.

CODY KIRSCH
Age 9

Just be quiet and wait for kids to come up to you. I made a lot of friends that way. There are some who are stuck up and conceited, but that's their problem.

SHAYNA OLSEN
Age 13

I was kind of shy and sat up by the window, and I didn't have a partner, and I was all alone. Then I came up to them and started playing. They played with me and smiled and stuff. Then I made more friends and was all better.

SASCHA GOLDHOR
Age 6

Don't stay in the library at recess or you'll be lonely. Instead, wear a smiling face and go play tetherball. Try not to be a goodie-goodie and show off, 'cause kids don't like that. Listen to their opinions and try not to be bossy. Smile all the time, and try to be nice and be considerate to them.

DAKOTA GOLDHOR
Age 10

Adjusting to "Culture Shock"

We live in an age when films, television, magazines, newspapers, books, and music reach the big city, the small city, the rural town, and the backwoods almost simultaneously. Geographic location doesn't mean what it used to mean a few decades ago. Unless you are moving to a truly remote area, total cultural deprivation is a thing of the past. The electronic and telecommunications revolution has made it possible for you to choose much of what you want from the popular culture no matter where you live.

What is different, however, is the pace at which people in smaller towns live and work. Time seems to slow down relative to the size of the community you move to.

Country people are reluctant to take to heart the fact that everything moves more slowly here. . . . We say the house will be built in three months when we mean four and a half. We say we'll be there in an hour when we mean more like two. Some things have to get done before the frost or the rains or whatever, and those are the things that get hurried along. But things where Nature is not involved . . . no. When you're on country time—Substandard Time—figure about 50 percent slower than Standard Time and you won't be disappointed.

FRANK KIRKPATRICK
*How to Find and Buy Your Business
in the Country*

Another common thing to expect after you arrive is long hours of work. It is the kind of work, however, that is very different from your former 60-hour fast-track workweek. The difference lies in the renewed vigor and endurance you gain from working at projects you thoroughly enjoy. You may find yourself puttering in a garden at dawn, working at your own business over the weekend, volunteering to drive the debate team to an out-of-town competition, participating on a local committee on a weeknight, moonlighting part-time as a musician, or doing any number of other activities that you have put on hold during your fast-track years.

WHAT TO DO WHEN THINGS GO WRONG

Any setbacks and disappointments should be regarded as part of the package deal, part of the process that will get you where you are going. Osel Tendzin discusses this idea in his book *Buddha in the Palm of Your Hand*:

> Having a proper attitude towards journey is essential. If we make a journey properly, then everything we encounter is considered part of it. We are fully involved in the process of journeying rather than being fixated on our destination. We are not looking for quick solutions, but are willing to be open, precise, and thorough in relating with ourselves as well as all the facets of our environment . . . and the obstacles or sidetracks along the way.

Expect that most setbacks will occur in the first several months. An essential part of your strategy should be to *keep an open mind*. You need to be flexible, curious, prepared for the unexpected, and willing to persevere through a change in circumstances. You also need to remain focused on your vision of the good life. Refer to the lists you composed in chapter 3. Keep your objectives in mind. Look at your overall plan of action, and at your longest-range goals—those 5 to 10 years away. Any temporary failure or misfortune will seem far less important when you're looking at the whole scheme of things, the big picture. Among the reasons people fail is the inability to see past tomorrow. Your long-range plan has a fair amount of give; any number of short-term goals can be forfeited without affecting the long-term.

> We tackled our practical problems one by one, as we reached them. In each case we followed a pattern which began with a survey of the situation, continued with a discussion or series of discussions which led to a decision, often written down in memorandum, black on white. The decision was elaborated into a plan, also written out and revised. Finally the plan was checked and coordinated with our ten year plan, adopted as a project and fitted into the work schedule. . . . Two people can accomplish much in a day or a month or a year if they have defined objectives,

agreed plans, if they work on the program systematically and conscientiously, giving as much attention to details as the overall plan.

Helen and Scott Nearing
Living the Good Life

Put Your Fears to Work for You

John D. Rockefeller was known for his ability to stick with his strategy. It seems he often did so more out of fear than anything else during the frenetic days when Standard Oil came into being. He would continually coach himself: "Your future hangs on every day that passes. . . . Look out, or you will lose your head—go steady."

In her book *Do What You Love, The Money Will Follow,* Marsha Sinetar suggests using misfortune, setbacks, and disappointments to trigger motivation:

> As a life-style, as a pattern of response, the best mechanism for reducing helplessness resides within us. We truly evolve and grow only when we take control of our circumstances and fears. While most people tend to regress to a state of feeling inadequate when they get anxious and scared, the truly resourceful person uses this as yet another opportunity to take charge of circumstances or events.

Let fear work for you. Anyone who has been up against a seemingly insurmountable deadline knows the value of this darker emotion! Don't be afraid to hope, to believe in your dream. Some former fast-trackers had to hit rock bottom before they could begin the climb back up. When the urge to panic rises, get out your long-range game plan and be bolstered by it.

Be Flexible

Having a proper attitude, having faith in yourself, and being able to use problems as opportunities to take control are all part of the formula for succeeding off the fast track.

When you come to the end of your rope, tie a knot and hang on.

Franklin D. Roosevelt

Gary Regester hung on through two very lean years when his primary source of income suddenly dried up. Throughout this period, he worked to develop a new prod-

uct line, and today he owns an international company manufacturing these products.

Don Smeller learned the hard way that in many rural areas work
shuts down for many tradesmen during the winter. While living in
Wenatchee, Washington, Don had to look to Seattle, a long distance
away, to find freelance work in the off-season. He remained flexible,
making himself available for spot jobs.

Keep an open mind to alternative ways of making a living and
meeting your needs. Coming into a new environment with unyield-
ing, preconceived notions will limit your opportunities.

For example, one alternative way to meet your needs is to use the
barter system.

> I do a fair amount of bartering. For example, I taught music at
> school in exchange for using the music facilities. I'm also working
> out a barter deal with one of the local ranchers who owns a
> taildragger airplane. The rancher has a pilot who can teach me to
> fly the plane. In exchange I'll fly for him for free for as many hours
> as it took to train me. Also, I worked as a medic at the Boy Scout
> camp in exchange for my son's going for free. Bartering comes in
> very handy around here!
>
> ELLEN KIMBLE
> *Marfa, Texas*

> We rely heavily on the barter system. I get my trucks repaired by a
> fella, and we keep his mules for him. I bartered the use of the
> stagecoach and horses for a wedding in exchange for having some
> accounting done.
>
> DON STEINMAN
> *Tucson, Arizona*

What is it you need? Find out who can answer the need. What
do you have to offer to exchange for what you need? It is better to offer something than to ask what they'll take instead of cash, which
puts the other person on the spot. Be sure that what you are offering is unique to you and not easy to get elsewhere. Whatever you exchange, write up a memo for both parties describing what it is and
how much.

Before we left the city, my husband and I were actively using
bartering skills. Todd exchanged commercial photography for sup-

plies: for example, he presented a barter proposal to a granite and marble company, offering to shoot the locations where they had their product exhibited. They could use the transparencies to do advertising, and in exchange they would supply and install granite countertops in our kitchen and marble in our bathroom. They were delighted with the proposal, and the deal worked without a hitch. We have since done similar barter deals for materials we would not otherwise have been able to afford.

> As for Olympic Lights [bed and breakfast] . . . it's beginning to pay its way, though Lea still tackles the odd freelance graphic assignment . . . and I still peddle papers. Besides the modest income, it involves me in the community. It even lets me practice a little bartering. I trade the unsold papers, which I'm entitled to keep, for firewood from an artisan nearby who uses them to wrap the dried flowers he sells by mail order. He has plenty of wood. Oak, madrona, Douglas fir. I have plenty of old newspaper and no wood. Voila! Exchanges like that happen all the time around here. People can make do without a whole lot of cash if they're careful and have something to offer.   (*Mother Earth News*, March, 1988)
>
> CHRISTIAN AND LEA ANDRADE
> *San Juan Island, Washington*

Toughing It Out

Remind yourself that you have chosen a life you can call your own. "Toughing it out" is a cruder way of saying *persevere*. Stay with it, and understand that every problem you encounter is part of the learning process. The more problems you solve, the better problem-solver you become. John Holt offered a new way of looking at this need for perseverance in his book *Never Too Late*. He emphasizes acceptance of the present, awareness of shortcomings, and keeping the goal in mind:

> Nothing is more conducive to happiness, than fixing on an end to be gained, and then steadily pursuing its attainment.
>
> J. C. LOUDON
> *An Encyclopedia of Agriculture*
> (1825)

> What I am slowly learning to do in my work with music is revive some of the resilience of the exploring and learning baby. I have to accept at each moment, as a fact of life, my present skill, and do the best I can, without blaming myself for not being able to do

better. I have to be aware of my mistakes and shortcomings without being ashamed of them. I have to keep in view the distant goal, without worrying about how far away it is or reproaching myself for not being already there. This is very hard for most adults. It is the main reason why we old dogs so often do find it so hard to learn new tricks, whether sports or languages or crafts or music. But if as we work on our skills we work on this weakness in ourselves, we can slowly get better at both.

You can extrapolate from Holt's lesson on learning and apply it to making your new life off the fast track work. You will have to sharpen certain skills and become more accomplished at them by making mistakes and learning from them.

Marsha Sinetar writes: "We need to have a real-life problem upon which to strengthen the muscles of our brain. Because success breeds success, the more we see ourselves as able to solve our most relevant concerns and get what we need for ourselves, the more trust we will have in our brains and the more resourceful we will become."

SETTLING IN TO THE GOOD LIFE

If you have made the move and have stuck with it, you will wake up one day and realize that you have arrived and survived! You have faced the trade-offs, changed your lifestyle, and chosen to do work that is more personally satisfying. As Joseph Campbell puts it, you

Success is going from failure to failure with great enthusiasm.

WINSTON CHURCHILL

As we change our habits and patterns, we realize that problems can teach us to grow. Yet because our problems are often painful and disturbing, our natural tendency is to try to avoid them; we seek ways to get out of difficult situations, or to go around the obstacles we encounter. But our problems are like clouds: though they appear to disturb the serenity of a clear sky, they contain life-giving moisture that nourishes growth. When we face our problems directly and go through them, we discover new ways of being. We build our strength and our confidence to deal with future difficulties. Life becomes a meaningful challenge leading us to greater knowledge and awakening. We discover that the more we learn, the more we grow; the more challenges we meet, the more strength and awareness we gain. When we live in accord with the process of change, we do something valuable simply by living.

TARTHANG TULKU
Skillful Means

have "followed your bliss." You have found that state of mind, that well-ordered inner harmony that comes from choosing to live with purpose, choosing to control your own destiny, and all the while staying true to your inner self.

I enjoy a repose to which I have been long a stranger. My mornings are devoted to correspondence. From breakfast to dinner, I am in my shops, my garden, or on horseback among my farms; from dinner to dark, I give to society and recreation with my neighbors and my friends; and from candle-light to early bedtime, I read. My health is perfect, and my strength considerably reinforced by the activity of the course I pursue; perhaps it is as great as usually falls to the lot of near 67 years of age. I talk of plows and harrows, of seeding and harvesting with my neighbors, and of politics, too, if they choose, with as little reserve as the rest of my fellow citizens, and feel, at length, the blessing of being free to say and do what I please, without being responsible to any mortal.

THOMAS JEFFERSON

We have not solved the problem of living. Far from it. But our experience convinces us that no family group possessing a normal share of vigor, energy, purpose, imagination and determination need continue to wear the yoke of a competitive, acquisitive, predatory culture. . . . The family can live with nature, make themselves a living that will preserve and enhance their efficiency, and give them leisure in which they can do their bit to make the world a better place.

HELEN AND SCOTT NEARING
Living the Good Life

SUGGESTED READING

CAMPBELL, JOSEPH. The Power of Myth. New York: Doubleday, 1988.

FIELDS, RICK, et al. Chop Wood, Carry Water. Los Angeles: Jeremy Tarcher, 1984.

KIRKPATRICK, FRANK. How to Find and Buy Your Business in the Country. Pownal, Vt.: Storey Communications, 1985.

LONG, CHARLES. Life after the City. Willowdale, Ontario Canada: Camden House, 1989.

NEARING, HELEN AND SCOTT. Living the Good Life. New York: Schocken Books, 1970.

Nozick, Robert. *The Examined Life.* New York: Simon and Schuster, 1989.

Peale, Norman Vincent. *The Power of Positive Thinking.* New York: Fawcett, 1978.

Sinetar, Marsha. *Do What You Love, The Money Will Follow.* New York: Dell Publishing, 1987.

Tendzin, Osel. *Buddha in the Palm of Your Hand.* Boston: Shambhala Publications, 1982.

Tulku, Tarthang. *Skillful Means.* Emeryville, Calif: Dharma Publishing, 1978.

7

If you cannot be free, be as free as you can.

EMERSON

If You Can't Get Out

Living the good life does not automatically mean stepping off the fast track. There is a wide variety of work and lifestyle alternatives from which to choose that can vastly improve the quality of your life. Never before in this country's history have there been so many opportunities to be free and independent in one's work. You don't necessarily have to work the daily grind, endure a long commute, arrive home in time for a frozen dinner and the late edition of the news, collapse in bed, and get up to face rush-hour traffic again a few hours later.

In the past few years there has been a steady migration away from full-time jobs in the city. An increasing number of people are choosing to work out of their homes, either for themselves or for an employer. For those who can't work at home and are eager for a change from the routine of their fast-track careers, there are several options to consider. As mentioned previously, many such options involve a simple step onto what Harvard Business School professor Leonard Schlesinger calls the "sanity track." Many younger executives, middle managers, and corporate executives are reconsidering the virtues of workaholism. Although some have decided to simply get out and start over, others have taken less drastic measures, such as cutting back work hours and turning down promotions.

Psychotherapist Stephen Price recently treated "an investment banker fed up with frequent trips abroad who quit for a business-school teaching job; a lawyer who felt so pressured 'he practically had a nervous breakdown' before finally accepting a much lower paying government job; and a television executive who turned down the chance to advance during a network shake-up. In the end he wanted time with his wife, time to read and garden at his country home, more than a promotion." (*Wall Street Journal*, June 13, 1989)

For those who crave what country living has to offer—fresh air, outdoor activities, starlit skies, peace and quiet, and a simpler way of life—but who can't relocate their work from the city, there are alternatives. For example, you could get away to the country for weekends or for an entire summer, or even commute from the city to the country on a daily basis. The sections that follow explore these alternatives.

WORK ALTERNATIVES

Cutting Back Work Hours and Business Travel

This is one of the easiest solutions for coping with out-of-control careerism. Robert Kelley, a business-school professor at Carnegie-Mellon University, believes the time has come when exhausting workweeks are no longer looked upon with respect and admiration: "There are enough very effective managers out there who are fed up with 60- to 70-hour workweeks. In the future, the very best managers will be those who keep their work lives under control, while the ones who brag about how much time they've spent at work will be viewed as disorganized."   (*Wall Street Journal*, June 13, 1988)

> Paul Whitehead, a 39-year-old attorney at the United Steelworkers union in Pittsburgh, has strong memories of "hearing the back door shut in our house every day at 4:52 P.M., hearing my dad walk into the front hall and kiss my mom hello. I associate my happy childhood with a father who was home." Mr. Whitehead used to routinely put in 70 hours a week at work. But since he married and subsequently had a son three years ago, he's learned to do more in fewer hours, so there's time left over for family. (*Wall Street Journal*, June 18, 1990)

David Machlowitz, a Manhattan attorney, exchanged 14-hour workdays and a partnership in his firm for a less-demanding corporate counsel's job. He chose the less-demanding job in order to spend more time with his wife.

Theresa Matsui struck a balance between her career as an engineer and her home life by rescheduling her work hours. She wanted to be home in time to relax before dinner with her husband and work in the garden before dusk. She leaves her office by 2:45 P.M. every day and beats rush-hour traffic out of Boston. She gets a bag lunch and picks up slack time over the noon hour. When she has work to make up, she compensates by getting to the office earlier in the morning. "Having that extra hour in the late afternoon is worth its weight in gold," she says.

Lateral Mobility

Lateral mobility, also called *plateauing*, means remaining at the same level of seniority but moving different places within the company. You can do this for several years or for the balance of a career. Lateral mobility offers several advantages, including a greater opportunity to learn other jobs and thus improve your skills and expertise.

A growing number of companies (among them, Monsanto, Pacific Gas and Electric, Motorola, General Electric, and Bell South) are implementing lateral mobility. By offering employees various alternatives to moving up in management, some companies are instituting a fellowship program which is similar to that in the university system, rewarding employees in non–fast track ways.

One reason that lateral mobility is a growing trend is that the definition of success—scaling the corporate ladder—has undergone a radical transformation in the past few years. It is no longer so much defined by what your title is and how much money you make. More and more, success is also measured by what kind of family man or woman you are and what other achievements you are proud of. Today, a person who balances work and home life is seen as a successful person.

Part-Time Work or Job-Sharing

Today, more women than men are looking for part-time work schedules to make time for raising a family. However, every year increasing numbers of men are also opting for this kind of change.

Judy Pesin, 38, used to work 12-hour workdays as a vice president of Citicorp. With the birth of her first child, she chose to work part time at the company. She says, "I'm good at what I do, but delivering $50 million in banker's acceptances isn't worth the trade-off" (*Wall Street Journal*, June 18, 1990).

Studies have shown that if you are a valued employee with a proven track record, you have an excellent chance of hammering out a part-time work schedule with your company or firm. An important key to getting your employer to agree to such a change is to spell out the benefits to the employer.

Stephanie Smith and her husband, both attorneys, felt that their jobs were robbing them of time with their 18-month-old son. "The pressures of meeting client demands and getting other things done in our lives meant life was exceedingly hectic," Stephanie says. Both proposed to their firms that they be allowed to work four-day weeks, with different days off, as an experiment. Both firms agreed. With plans to have a second child, Stephanie started working three days a week, switching over to management and policy issues. During her maternity leave, her firm made her a partner. Other attorneys in her firm have taken the cue, cutting back work hours in order to spend more time with their families (*Los Angeles Times*, May 12, 1989).

Job-sharing is another option that offers a solution to the individual who can neither work full time at home nor full time at the office and has difficulty working out a part-time work schedule.

Gay Geiser-Sandoval suggested sharing a job as a deputy district attorney with a partner of hers in Orange County, California. Gay, a mother of two, needed more time for her family without sacrificing her work. She and her partner, also a mother, presented a proposal that persuaded the district attorney's office of the benefits of their plan. They presented details of how they would split the workload, and they included an agreement to cover for each other when either took time off. Both offered to be on call in the event that the office needed them. They pointed out the real benefit of avoiding burnout on the job, and the subjective benefit of having happier employees. They suggested that their proposal be used as a pilot program for 6 to 12 months. The arrangement was accepted, and it has proved to be a big success.

Working at Home for Your Current Employer

This alternative offers what some feel is security in their jobs, but without the supervision of their bosses as they work in the relaxed, comfortable atmosphere of home.

More and more corporations are allowing their employees the chance to work at home a few days a week. The employees enjoy the flexibility, and the corporations are able to hold on to valuable employees and attract the best applicants. Companies are also discovering that part-time employees experience increased productivity when working at home, because they are able to concentrate better and to work for longer periods of time without office interruptions. In two different studies of state-employed telecommuters and corporate telecomuters, personal productivity often increased by as much as 15%.

Pacific Bell is an example of a company that has encouraged its employees in this direction—more than 500 of its current employees work two or three days a week at home. Such companies provide the computers and the software that make at-home work possible, believing the investment to be more than worthwhile.

Later in this chapter is a section on the pros and cons of working at home, which provides some tips for doing so successfully.

Switching Employers

If one of the options above seems attractive to you, yet your employer is unsympathetic, you might consider switching employers. In doing so, first call around to discover which potential employers already have flexible work options. When you interview for a new job, be upfront about the work alternatives you are interested in and give that as the reason you are leaving your other job. As mentioned before, the key to getting your work alternative accepted is to convince the employer of the benefits to the company.

Some fast-trackers switch employers in order to do work that is more personally fulfilling and makes a contribution to society. Ralph Urban is a 33-year-old lawyer from East Hampton, Connecticut, who formerly worked for a Hartford law firm. He chose to take a $15,000 pay cut to work as an assistant attorney general for the state. "I wanted to do something more in the public interest. You can't put a monetary value on the satisfaction you get from your work," he said in the *Hartford Advocate* (May 21, 1990). His wife, also an attorney, works part time in order to care for their young son. They compensate for their drop in income by living a more frugal lifestyle.

Switching Careers

If none of the options above is available to you in your current career, you may want to make a career change without uprooting.

Ted Schmitt left a six-figure income in financial public relations to become a producer and artistic director of the Cast Theater in Hollywood. "I sacrificed a real comfortable situation. . . . I now live in a small apartment in Hollywood, and drive a 1965 Mustang. . . . But I regained my soul" (*Los Angeles Times*, November 27, 1987).

Robert Badal quit his job as a commodities broker and today conducts seminars on a variety of subjects at a dozen or so colleges and institutions. He also sells rare coins, teaches an aerobic class, and sends out two newsletters, one on romance and the other on financial advice. "It's great—I'm getting paid to do all the things I love." He recommends that the person trying to go freelance for the first time line up several part-time sources of income, since the first year is often the hardest (*Los Angeles Times*, November 27, 1987).

Both of these individuals switched careers in order to do work that was more personally satisfying. In both their cases, it meant earning less money but remaining in the city. Michael Phillips wrote about this growing phenomenon in the *Briarpatch Book*:

> In the past it was considered reasonable for people to develop a marketable skill and pursue a career that would earn them enough money to do the things they really wanted to do. People worked at their jobs so they could do the things they wanted on weekends, go where they wanted on vacations and, in some cases, earn enough to retire "early" and then do what they wanted. Now our peers are saying, "that's nonsense; why should I do something I don't like 70% of my life so I can do what I want 30%?" The old wage-slave mentality of renting ourselves to our jobs for eight hours a day to cover the essentials of life is giving way to the awareness that work is an integral part of our lives. Therefore the quality of our lives and the quality of our work-time are one and the same.

Starting a Business or Freelancing

More than one-third of the entrepreneurs in this country work at home. More than a quarter of those in the work force have shifted all or part of their jobs to the home front. What many are after is the dream of integrating their home and their office, their family and their work, and their relationships and themselves geographically, emotionally, and psychologically.

Another factor in this shift is the loss of job security in today's merger-madness atmosphere, where employees are no longer considered permanent and valuable assets. The security of long-term company careers is a thing of the past.

According to the American Home Business Association, approximately 27 million Americans—1 in 10—work out of their homes either full time or part time. This includes about 13 million business owners who work full time out of their homes, about 3 million employees whose firms allow them to work full time at home, and about 11 million people who work part time at home.

Working at home has become possible for a wide range of businesses because of vastly improved communication systems, personal computers, overnight delivery, fax machines, modems, scanners, and call-waiting. At-home businesses are considered no less professional or profitable than office-based businesses.

Industries that were formerly off-limits to freelancers—for example, banking, insurance, entertainment, and advertising—are now offering a flood of opportunities.

> Across the country, in Madison, Connecticut, Bonnie Figett, another working mother, commutes to work 20 feet each morning from her kitchen to her study. Bonnie does industry analysis for the Travelers Insurance Company by connecting her computer to the company's mainframe computer in Hartford. For Bonnie, the joys of telecommuting are working alone, which she likes. And although her children are out of the house all day, they are nearby. And there's one more plus: only once a week does Bonnie face the 30-mile commute to Hartford.   (NBC News, July 18, 1990)

Kemp Battle was an international trader in his early thirties who quit his job after being unhappy for several months. He started his own company as an investment-banking consultant, working out of an office close to his home. He gave up job security and the camaraderie of his former peers. In exchange, however, he experienced "a 180-degree change in the bond I feel with my family. . . . I can pick my daughter up from school and drop her home—and have more contact doing that than I used to have in a week" (Wall Street Journal, June 13, 1989).

Sonny Harris worked as a middle manager at a Fortune 500 company for a number of years, surviving staff reductions and department mergers. He says, "I didn't want to be 100% dependent on my employer, having it be my sole source of income. I wanted to make choices and not have some committee deciding for me." While in his mid-thirties. Harris began purchasing rental properties, working on them in his free time and renting them out to pay the overhead. He also began preparations to buy into a small diner. During this time he continued working for the same employer. Before he turned 45, he was offered an early retirement package, which he jumped at. His income today is only a third of what he used to make on the fast track, and he works more hours than he did before, yet he is happy. "I feel an exhilarating sense of freedom every day just knowing that I'm in charge. I make my own choices—I'm at the helm!"

As discussed in chapter 4, a good place to start if one is considering starting a business is to look to former employers. Can you offer a service to them as a freelance contractor? A large number of people step off the fast track by starting up consultation businesses, with former employers on the client list. Tom Kosnik is leaving Harvard Business School, where he was a professor putting in a 75-hour workweek, to become a part-time consultant and writer.

There are hundreds of options, depending on your skills and expertise. Most professionals can become a one-person business provided there exists a demand for their services. Or, you could buy into an existing retail or wholesale business, or perhaps a franchise, if you think you have the skills to make it a success. Refer to chapter 4 for a more thorough discussion of the opportunities and directions to consider in starting or developing your own business.

THE PROS AND CONS OF WORKING AT HOME

Many of the work alternatives just discussed involve working at home, which, as we have seen, is an increasingly attractive option for many. There are, however, both advantages and disadvantages to working at home.

THE ADVANTAGES

- *Having low overhead.*

    You are not paying any office rent. The initial cost of setting up a home business will be the cost of your telecommunications equipment: your computer, printer, copying machine, fax machine, extra phone lines, and so on—all of which are tax-deductible. If you are frugal, you can set up a complete home office for somewhere between $5,000 and $10,000. You save on gasoline because you no longer have to commute, and on the wear and tear on your car. You also save on the cost of your annual business wardrobe.

- *Being at home with your family.*

   A growing number of working parents view child-rearing duties as both an emotional and psychological imperative. They do not want to hire help to feed their children, to take them to school, or to babysit them during the day while Mom and Dad are out earning a living. The desire to nurture their own makes working at home seem even more worthwhile. It is not only children that have stirred familial passions. More and more businesspeople are finding that they miss spending time with their spouses. Working at home gives them what they once looked upon as a luxury.

- *Avoiding traffic and long commutes.*

- *Escaping office politics, gossip, and interruptions.*

- *Being in control of your own time.*

- *Developing intimacy between work and your life.*

- *Dressing casually.*

- *Eating meals with family members.*

- *Having variety in the daily routine.*

The Disadvantages

- *Having too many family interruptions.*

- *Not having adequate supplies and equipment.*

- *Missing interaction with co-workers, the exchange of ideas, the office politics and gossip.*

- *Not being able to work without a structured routine: losing discipline.*

- *Having too many household chores.*

- *Needing the direction of a boss.*

- *Needing a change in environment.*

- *Putting too much emphasis on work.*

The need for balance between work and domestic life is crucial, as many home workers have learned. An imbalance either way creates its own set of problems: work doesn't get done, or a peaceful hearth is upset.

TIPS FOR WORKING AT HOME

What makes the ideal at-home worker? The following traits were most often mentioned by a variety of full-time and part-time at-home workers:

- Likes to take the initiative.
- Is self-managed.
- Not afraid to be isolated from co-workers or the work environment.
- Likes to be in control of his or her own destiny.
- Is optimistic and self-confident.

The following tips can help you increase your chances for success in working at home:

1. Dress for work. Lose the bathrobe. Dress as if a client might drop in unexpectedly.

2. Use a separate room for the office. Don't set up shop in the way of domestic traffic. If you don't have the luxury of a separate room, create a business "zone" using bookcases, plants, file cabinets—whatever is available that helps define your business space, keeping it apart from the household.

3. If you share child-rearing duties, schedule your work hours around time spent with the children. This may require that work hours are decided by naptimes and bedtimes. It requires a willing spouse prepared to spend as much time with the kids as he/she spends with work. More and more couples are doing without child care for their infants and young children as they are willing to work nontraditional hours—starting at dawn, maybe working late into the evening. Some say it can be round-the-clock chores, yet few of these couples complain, as they consider it a luxury to work at home and care for their own children.

4. Keep personal calls for after hours. You can do this three ways: screen calls coming in on an answering machine—pick up business, call back personals after hours; install two phone lines—keep business for one number and have a service or answering machine pick up the personal line when you are at work; if a

personal call comes in during work hours, tell the caller you are at work and will call back at an agreed-upon time.

5. Prepare in advance for all household interruptions. Discuss with your spouse and children what qualifies as an emergency. Decide in advance who picks up the kids, unloads the washing machine, feeds the dog. You can leave a note to have deliveries dropped at the front door. Hold off reading the mail and the morning paper until after work hours.

6. Avoid visiting the office after work hours. It encourages bad habits that lead to workaholism, and it also gives you an excuse to cut designated work hours because you can "do it later."

7. Save the grocery shopping, the laundry, the house repairs, and the like for the weekend or after hours.

8. Make contact every day with another business associate, client, or co-worker.

9. Plan a trip to the bank, the post office, the stationery store—one business-related outing at least every other day to keep you from the "vegetation blues."

10. Keep business-related correspondence, overnight mail, and faxes in your office. Don't mix business bills with household bills. Make it clear to family members which are home phones and which are business phones.

11. Don't eat your meals in the office and don't call an associate from the bedroom.

12. Don't try to regiment your workday as you did at the office, namely working from 9 to 5. The reason you are at home is because of the flexibility it affords you. Take advantage of it.

13. Set goals for each workday. Stick to your deadlines. Once you begin procrastinating and putting off work, it can become irresistably addictive.

LIFESTYLE ALTERNATIVES

If you are eager to escape the drawbacks of your fast-track career but do not want to quit your job or alter your work situation, another possibility is to change your lifestyle. The following alternatives can help you create the kind of atmosphere that is conducive to fuller, simpler living.

Commute from the Country

This option is usually chosen by individuals living outside smaller cities. Many who have tried it in New York City and Los Angeles discover that too long a commute can create its own problems and defeat the purposes for which the move was made. Some who have tried it in larger cities combine it with one of the above-mentioned work alternatives—for example, they commute perhaps three days a week spending two workdays at home. An already flexible work schedule can free you up to move farther outside the city, provided you don't mind the longer commute fewer times a week.

For nearly 10 years, Donna and Jim Onstott endured nearly an hour-long commute each way to their jobs in St. Paul, Minnesota, from an old farmhouse they had renovated in the country. Finally, they decided to move closer to the city. They sold their farmhouse and bought a farm in western Wisconsin, closer to St. Paul. Their new home fits all their criteria: open land for horses, protection from nearby development, open country for hiking and cross-country skiing, and, of course, a reasonable (30-minute) commute into the city.

> Shortly after coming home from work one Friday night, Jim heads down to the barn. He flips on the lights and greets the horses, who are waiting. The sheep are huddled together against the December cold. . . . Jim gives the horses a few buckets of grain, tosses the sheep several flakes of hay, and fills the dogs' bowl with food. . . . The house, its lights glowing yellow on the hillside, is visible through an open door. The scene is one of rural contentment, far removed in time and place from traffic jams and high technology. That is just how the Onstotts like it. (*Harrowsmith,* March, 1988)

Another way of commuting is by airplane. A growing number of business executives and professional people are taking advantage of the best of both worlds—keeping their jobs in the city and their homes 1,000 or more miles away in the mountains or on the range. Popular places that people are choosing to commute from include Park City, Utah; Vail, Colorado; and Santa Fe, New Mexico. Most keep an apartment in the city, where they work three-or four days a week before flying home for a three- or four-day weekend.

> With the mountain sun filtering through cottonwood trees and chamisa bushes, businessman and writer Christopher Leinberger rises at dawn, walks the dogs, feeds the chickens, puts his five

horses out to pasture and heads for his office on Wilshire Boulevard—more than 1,000 miles away. Flying in from Albuquerque, Leinberger spends two days a week in Los Angeles running his real estate consulting firm. (*Los Angeles Times*, October 29, 1989)

Spend Weekends or Time Off in the Country

Some people find that getting away to the country on the weekends provides them with all the rejuvenation they need. On Monday morning they're secure in the knowledge that Friday afternoon will find them once more heading for the country.

Sarah and Conner Shanahan both work full time in Los Angeles in the advertising industry. They have arranged their work schedules so that they can leave Los Angeles before 3 P.M. on Fridays (in order to beat the traffic heading east out of the city) and drive two hours to Lake Arrowhead in the San Bernardino Mountains. There, they own a cabin on a dirt road that adjoins the national forest. "We rarely have a car drive by on the weekends—even the holidays," says Sarah. "We buy our groceries Friday evening and head back to our hideaway, where we read, cook, cut firewood, work in the garden, and do pretty much what everyone else living in the country does—except watch TV. The drive up the mountain, up through the smog to clear blue skies, is reason enough to justify the commute. We breathe in fresh clean air, swim at the lake, or go down to Deep Creek in the national forest. We restore our spirits and are ready for another five days in the rat race. We enjoy the best of city and country living, never taking either of them for granted."

Michelle Daniels works as a freelance writer, which affords her the opportunity to commute from her hideaway in the country, spending weeks in San Francisco and weeks in the country. She keeps an inexpensive apartment in the city. She says, "I've nearly paid off the house, although it has been month-to-month living. I am 42 and live pretty frugally. I thought about living here full time but have discovered that I appreciate it a lot more when I spend a week or more a month in the city. My work remains steady, though that can change tomorrow. I love my life as it is now part time in the city and part time in the country."

If you cannot afford a hideaway in the country, there are many ways to get away for a weekend and go hiking or camping. Terry and Susan Demmings set aside one weekend a month for an excursion into the country. One month may be a weekend hiking in New York's

Adirondack Park; the next month may be river rafting on the Colorado River. They claim that the anticipation they feel for each monthly outing keeps them content the other three weeks in the city.

Take Summers Off

This may require some liberal consideration on the part of your employer. Present a proposal that will demonstrate how you plan to accomplish a year's work in nine months. Set a quota or some other measure of your work that you intend to meet by year's end. Explain that you want two or three consecutive months when you will not be coming into the office. If need be, you can offer to work extra hours during the week, perhaps work one weekend a month, and take less time off on regularly scheduled days off and vacations. If necessary, suggest that you will be able to take a limited amount of work with you when you take off for the summer. As mentioned before, you will need to show how your work plan will provide definite benefits for your employer.

If you are self-employed, set up a rigorous work schedule for nine months of the year that will allow you to take the summers off.

Taking the summer off can be rewarding if you have school-age children who are free during the summer.

Simplify Your Live

In 1936, Richard Gregg, a Harvard-educated disciple of Mahatma Gandhi, published an essay called "*The Value of Voluntary Simplicity.*" That essay has greatly influenced the trend in recent years toward doing away with superfluities. Gregg wrote, "Voluntary simplicity . . . means singleness of purpose, sincerity, and honesty within, as well as avoidance of exterior clutter, or many possessions irrelevant to the chief purpose of life." There was, he said, one important condition of simple living to keep in mind. He explained it by referring to a discussion he had had with Gandhi:

> We were talking about simple living, and I said that it was easy for me to give up most things but that I had a greedy mind and wanted to keep my many books. He said, "Then don't give them up. As long as you derive inner help and comfort from anything, you should keep it. If you were to give it up in a mood of self-sacrifice or out of a stern sense of duty, you would continue to want it back, and that unsatisfied want would make trouble for

you. Only give up a thing when you want some other condition so much that the thing no longer has any attraction for you, or when it seems to interfere with that which is more greatly desired.

There are many ways to simplify your life—spiritual, practical, psychological, environmental, philosophical. The key to living simply is *moderation in all that you do.*

As we saw earlier in this book, many ex-FTers felt that their lives had become too complex. While you, the reader, may find your life is also complex in many ways, you may not wish to make as drastic a move in your career or in where you live. Here are a few examples of how others like you found ways to simplify their work and their family life.

Work

- Cutting back on business travel.
- Foregoing cocktail parties and dinners that are business-related.
- Not working on the weekends.
- Scheduling work hours to be home in time for dinner with the family.

Family

- Limiting the number of sports, lessons, classes, and club and other social functions.
- Setting aside one day a week for the family to be together.

Many discovered that by eliminating various activities, they could better appreciate and concentrate on the few they chose to do. They discovered that freeing up more time gave them the freedom to choose what they wanted to do—a freedom many said they had never before felt. They experienced the luxury of living simpler lives.

To live the simple life in the city may seem more difficult than in a rural area because of the chaos, noise, and freneticism. But it doesn't have to be so. William Whyte has written a "love song" to the city in a book called *City.* In the book, he urges city dwellers to cherish all that is good in our cities, *including* its chaos and its eccentricities.

> 'Tis the gift to be simple, 'Tis the gift to be free . . .
>
> *Shaker hymn from the early 1800s*

Some of the simplest lives are lived in the city. You can spot a few at the library, at the park, and down at the museum watching and enjoying humanity in its most intimate surroundings.

SUGGESTED READING

EDWARDS, PAUL AND SARAH. *Working from Home: Everything You Need to Know about Living and Working under the Same Roof.* Los Angeles: J. P. Tarcher, 1985.

ELGIN, DUANE, and MITCHELL, ARNOLD. "Voluntary Simplicity: Life-Style of the Future." *Futurist* II (1977):200–209.

GREGG, RICHARD. *The Value of Voluntary Simplicity.* Wallingford, Pa.: Pendle Hill, 1936.

LEVINSON, JAY. *Earning Money Without a Job: The Economics of Freedom.* New York: Holt Rinehart Winston, 1979.

LONG, CHARLES. *How to Survive Without a Salary.* Toronto: Summerhilll Press, 1988.

NEARING, HELEN AND SCOTT. *Living the Good Life.* New York: Schocken Books, 1970.

OLMSTED, BARNEY, and SMITH, SUZANNE. *Creating a Flexible Workplace: How to Select and Manage Alternative Work Options.* San Francisco: American Management Assoc. (New Ways to Work), 1989.

———. *The Job-Sharing Handbook.* Berkeley: Ten Speed Press, 1983.

PHILLIPS, MICHAEL. The Briarpatch Community. *The Briarpatch Book.* New Glide/Reed, 1975.

RUBIN, BONNIE. *Time Out.* New York: W. W. Norton, 1987.

SHI, DAVID E. *In Search of the Simple Life.* Salt Lake City: Peregrine Smith, 1986.

WHYTE, WILLIAM H. *City.* New York: Doubleday, 1988.

> [I]f you do follow your bliss you put yourself on a kind of track that has been there all the while, waiting for you, and the life that you ought to be living is the one you are living. When you can see that, you begin to meet people who are in the field of your bliss, and they open the doors to you. I say, follow your bliss and don't be afraid, and doors will open where you didn't know they were going to be. . . . Wherever you are—if you are following your bliss, you are enjoying that refreshment, that life within you, all the time.
>
> JOSEPH CAMPBELL

Epilogue: What Money Can't Buy

Looking to restore meaning and fullness in their lives, many people today are synthesizing the practical and the spiritual, the mechanistic and the humanistic. They seek to make their jobs more satisfying, to spend more time with family and friends, and to savor the simple joys in life. They yearn to find balance, a measure of personal peace. They feel the need to help others, to conserve and protect the natural beauty of the world. For those who leave the fast track behind, the rewards are far beyond anything that money can buy.

By now, you, too, have developed a personal vision of the good life and a plan of action to make it a reality. As it does for others, for you that decision may mean making sacrifices, working hard, and persevering through unexpected adversity. But it will also guarantee an immeasurable return on your time, energy, and resources. You will discover the certain pleasure that comes from controlling your destiny, choosing to live your life as your inner self directs you, and meeting life's challenges and opportunities armed with vitality, a strong belief in yourself, and a respect and sense of wonder for the world around you. Few, if any, regret the decision to step off the fast track. The quest for the good life becomes the adventure of a lifetime.

If you have decided to count yourself among this privileged group, you will have answered the questions honestly, you will have made the difficult decisions, and you will have taken the first crucial steps toward making it all happen. I wish you luck—though I don't believe you'll need it!

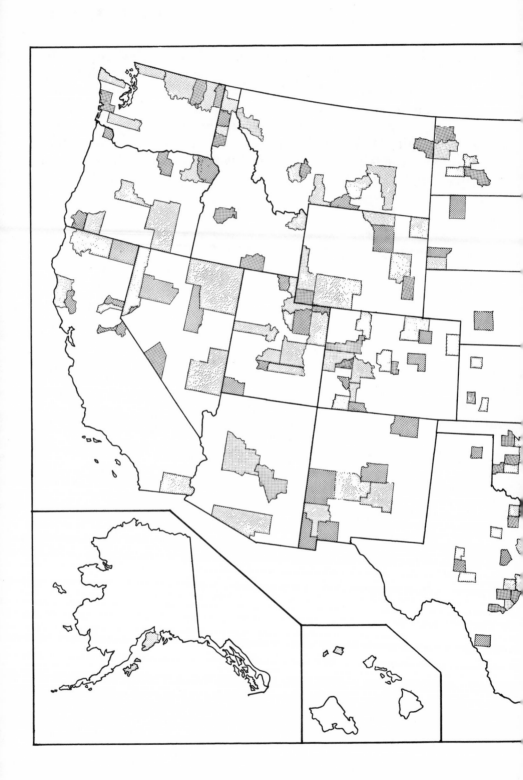

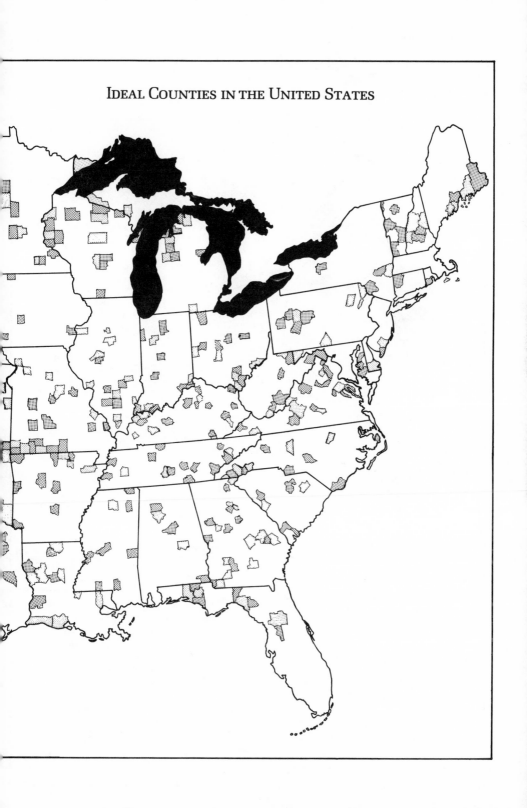

IDEAL COUNTIES IN THE UNITED STATES

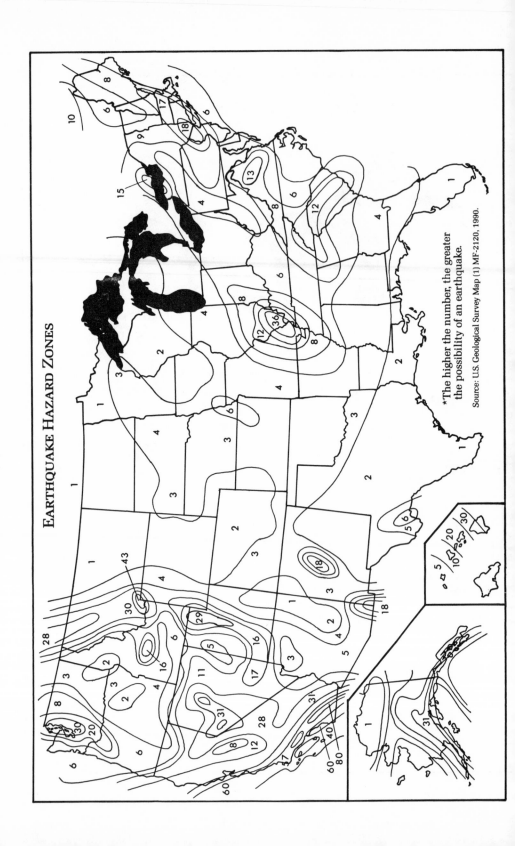

EARTHQUAKE HAZARD ZONES

*The higher the number, the greater the possibility of an earthquake.

Source: U.S. Geological Survey Map (1) MF-2120, 1990.

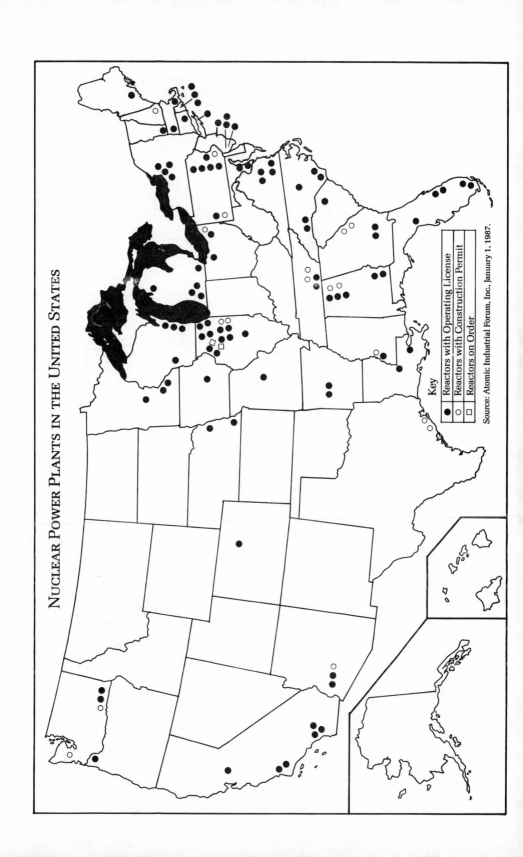

NUCLEAR POWER PLANTS IN THE UNITED STATES

Key

● Reactors with Operating License
○ Reactors with Construction Permit
□ Reactors on Order

Source: Atomic Industrial Forum, Inc., January 1, 1987.

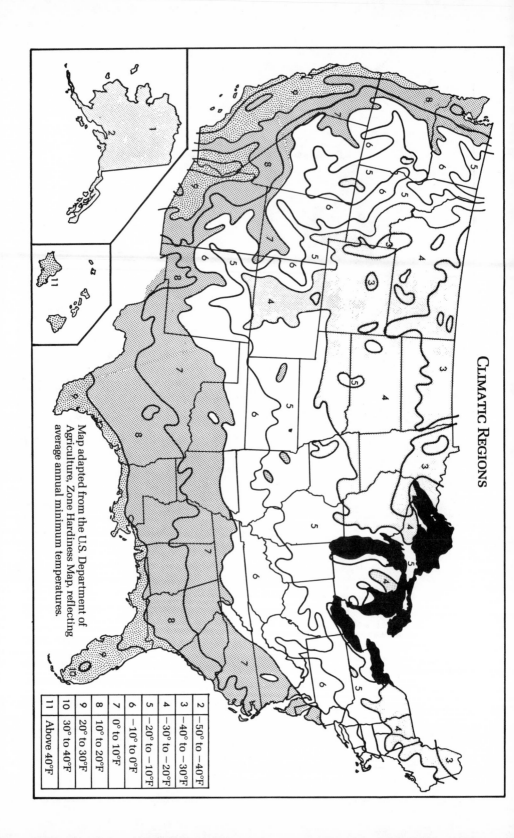

CLIMATIC REGIONS

Map adapted from the U.S. Department of
Agriculture, Zone Hardiness Map, reflecting
average annual minimum temperatures.

2	−50° to −40°F
3	−40° to −30°F
4	−30° to −20°F
5	−20° to −10°F
6	−10° to 0°F
7	0° to 10°F
8	10° to 20°F
9	20° to 30°F
10	30° to 40°F
11	Above 40°F

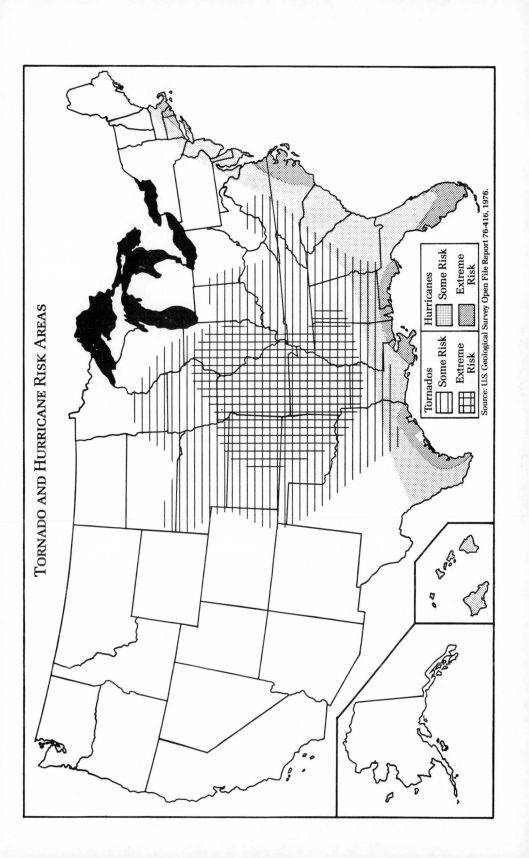

TORNADO AND HURRICANE RISK AREAS

Tornados
Some Risk
Extreme Risk

Hurricanes
Some Risk
Extreme Risk

Source: U.S. Geological Survey Open File Report 76-416, 1976.

Ideal Counties in the United States

Alabama

Elmore
Houston
Shelby
Walker
Winston

Alaska

Kenai Peninsula
Kodiak Island

Arizona

Gila
Pima
Yavapai

Arkansas

Baxter
Benton
Craighead
Faulkner
Fulton
Grant
Little River
Pope
Sebastian
Sharp

California

Alpine
Amador
Imperial
Lake
Mendocino
Modoc
Nevada
Sierra
Siskiyou

Colorado

Archuleta
Delta
Elbert
Garfield
Gunnison
Hinsdale

La Plata
Mesa
Morgan
Ouray
Park
Routt
Teller
Weld
Yuma

Connecticut
Litchfield

Delaware
Sussex

Florida
Bay
Holmes
Jefferson
Lafayette
Marion
Sumter
Taylor
Walton
Washington

Georgia
Barrow
Bulloch
Chandler
Coffee
Coweta
Decatur
Emanuel
Harris
Laurens
Lee
Mitchell

Monroe
Oconee
Pike
Putnam
Rabun
Seminole
Walton
White
Worth

Hawaii
Kauai

Idaho
Benewah
Boise
Bonner
Cassia
Fremont
Kootenai
Latah

Illinois
Bond
Cumberland
Edwards
Effingham
Jefferson
Jersey
Johnson
Marion
Mason
Menard
Mercer
Putnam
Washington
Williamson
Woodford

Indiana
Boone
Dearborn
Fulton
Jefferson
Marshall
Newton
Ohio
Owen
Posey
Spencer
Warrick
White

Iowa
Dallas
Dickinson
Louisa
Mills

Kansas
Butler
Gray
Harvey
Jefferson
Kearny
Miami
Pottawatomie
Thomas

Kentucky
Breathitt
Clark
Grant
Grayson
Greenup
Hopkins
Henderson
Johnson

Lyon
Muhlenberg
Perry
Scott
Shelby
Union
Webster
Whitley
Woodford

Louisiana

Beauregard
Cameron
De Soto
Grant
La Salle
Lincoln
Natchitoches
Sabine
Tangipahoa
Union
Vermilion
West Feliciana

Maine

Hancock
Knox
Lincoln
Waldo
Washington

Maryland

Garrett
Queen Annes
Talbot
Worcester

Massachusetts

Dukes
Nantucket

Michigan

Antrim
Arenac
Cheboygan
Dickinson
Emmet
Gogebic
Grand Traverse
Hillsdale
Lake
Leelanau
Osceola
Wexford

Minnesota

Becker
Cook
Dodge
Kandiyohi
Meeker
Otter Tail
Steele
Todd
Wabasha

Mississippi

Alcorn
Lafayette
Lamar
Lauderdale
Lee
Madison
Pike
Warren

Missouri

Andrew
Barry

Benton
Callaway
Cape Girardeau
Christian
Clinton
Cole
Howell
Laclede
Madison
McDonald
Newton
Ozark
Polk
Randolph
Ray
Ste. Genevieve
Stone
Taney
Warren

Montana

Broadwater
Carbon
Jefferson
Park
Richland
Rosebud
Sanders
Yellowstone

Nebraska

Box Butte
Cass
Dakota
Lincoln
Madison
Stanton
Washington

Nevada
Elko
Esmeralda
Eureka
Lincoln
Pershing
Storey
Washoe

New Hampshire
Belknap
Carroll
Grafton
Merrimack
Sullivan

New Jersey
Atlantic
Cape May

New Mexico
Catron
Colfax
Grant
Hidalgo
Lincoln
Luna
Socorro
Torrance

New York
Columbia
Greene
Ontario
Sullivan

North Carolina
Brunswick

Chowan
Clay
Dare
Davie
Iredell
Jackson
Henderson
Macon
Moore
Nash
Transylvania
Union

North Dakota
Cass
McKenzie
Mercer
Morton
Stark
Williams

Ohio
Darke
Fulton
Gallia
Holmes
Jackson
Laurence
Madison
Morrow
Shelby
Union
Vinton
Washington

Oklahoma
Beckham
Blaine
Canadian

Carter
Creek
Custer
Delaware
Garfield
Grady
Logan
Love
Major
Marshall
McCurtain
Noble
Osage
Ottawa
Pawnee
Pottawatomie
Pushmataha
Stephens
Wagoner
Washita
Woodward

Oregon
Columbia
Deschutes
Harney
Jackson
Josephine
Morrow
Union
Wallowa

Pennsylvania
Butler
Clarion
Clearfield
Franklin
Indiana
Jefferson

Wayne
Wyoming

Rhode Island

Washington

South Carolina

Beaufort
Darlington
Edgefield
Greenwood
Hampton
Kershaw

South Dakota

Custer
Fall River
Lincoln
Perkins

Tennessee

Bedford
Bledsoe
Cannon
Dickson
Dyer
Jefferson
Madison
Marion
Marshall
Monroe
Robertson
Sevier
Tipton
Union

Texas

Anderson
Archer
Austin
Bandera
Bastrop
Blanco
Brown
Burnet
Camp
Clay
Dimmit
Ellis
Erath
Freestone
Gillespie
Hood
Irion
Kaufman
Kendall
Llano
Madison
Matagorda
Nacogdoches
Navarro
Rains
Roberts
Schleicher
Shackelford
Somervell
Sterling
Titus
Upshur
Waller
Washington
Williamson
Wise
Wood
Young

Utah

Cache
Duchesne
Emery
Juab
Piute
Rich
Sevier
Summit
Uintah
Wasatch
Washington
Wayne

Vermont

Addison
Bennington
Grand Isle
Lamoille
Windsor

Virginia

Alleghany
Appomattox
Augusta
Bedford
Botetourt
Caroline
Clarke
Essex
Fauquier
Franklin
Goochland
Greene
King William
Middlesex
Orange
Prince Edward
Rappahannock

Washington
Wise

Washington

Clallam
Ferry
Grays Harbor
Lewis
Okanogan
Pend Oreille
Stevens
Whatcom

West Virginia

Berkeley
Greenbrier
Hampshire

Jefferson
Mercer
Monongalia
Morgan
Preston
Summers
Upshur

Wisconsin

Adams
Burnett
Door
Dunn
Florence
Green
Marathon
Marquette

Oneida
Pierce
Polk
St. Croix
Sawyer
Waushara
Vilas

Wyoming

Converse
Crook
Johnson
Lincoln
Platte
Sheridan
Sweetwater
Uinta

State Chambers of Commerce

Alabama
41 Commerce Street
Montgomery, AL 36101
Phone: 205-834-5200

Alaska
217 2nd Street, #201
Juneau, AK 99801
Phone: 907-586-2323

Arizona
1221 East Osborn Road, #100
Phoenix, AZ 85014
Phone: 602-248-9172

Arkansas
410 South Cross
Little Rock, AR 72201
Phone: 501-374-9225

California
1201 K Street
P.O. Box 1736
Sacramento, CA 95812-1736
Phone: 916-444-6670

Colorado
1445 Market Street
Denver, CO 80202
Phone: 303-534-8500

Connecticut
250 Constitution Plaza
Hartford, CT 06103
Phone: 203-525-4451

Delaware
1 Commerce Center, #200
Wilmington, DE 19801
Phone: 302-655-7221

Florida
1601 Biscayne Boulevard
Miami, FL 33132
Phone: 305-350-7700

Georgia
Box 1740
Atlanta, GA 30301
Phone: 404-880-9000

Hawaii
735 Bisop Street
Honolulu, HI 96813
Phone: 808-522-8800

Idaho
Box 2368
300 N. 6th Street
Boise, ID 83707
Phone: 208-344-5515

Illinois
20 North Wacker Drive
Chicago, IL 60606
Phone: 312-372-7373

Indiana
1 N. Capital, #700
Indianapolis, IN 46204
Phone: 317-232-8800

Iowa
309 Court Avenue, #300
Des Moines, IA 50309
Phone: 515-286-4950

Kansas
500 Bank 4 Tower
Topeka, KS 66603
Phone: 913-357-6321

Kentucky
Box 817
Frankfort, KY 40602
Phone: 502-695-4700

Louisiana
Box 3217
Baton Rouge, LA 70821
Phone: 504-381-7125

Maine
142 Free Street
Portland, ME 04101
Phone: 207-772-2811

Maryland
275 West Street, #400
Annapolis, MD 21401
Phone: 301-269-0642

Massachusetts
600 Atlantic Avenue, 13th Floor
Boston, MA 00210-2200
Phone: 617-227-4500

Michigan
Box 30226
Lansing, MI 48909
Phone: 517-373-1700

Minnesota
445 Minnesota Street, #600
St. Paul, MN 55101
Phone: 612-223-5000

Mississippi
Box 23276
Jackson, MS 39225-3276
Phone: 601-969-0022

Missouri
10 S. Broadway, #300
St. Louis, MO 63102
Phone: 800-247-9791

Montana
Box 1730
Helena, MT 59624
Phone: 406-442-2405

Nebraska
Box 95128
Lincoln, NE 68509
Phone: 402-474-4422

Nevada
Box 3499
Reno, NV 89505
Phone: 702-329-3558

New Hampshire
889 Elm Street
Manchester, NH 03101
Phone: 603-666-6600

New Jersey
40 Clinton Street
Newark, NJ 07102
Phone: 201-242-6237

New Mexico
Box 1395
Gallup, NM 87305
Phone: 505-722-2228

New York
518 Broadway
Albany, NY 12207
Phone: 518-434-1214

North Carolina
Box 2978
Raleigh, NC 27602
Phone: 919-833-3005

North Dakota
321 4th Street N.
Fargo, ND 58102
Phone: 701-237-5678

Ohio
35 E. Gay Street, 2nd Floor
Columbus, OH 43215-3181
Phone: 614-228-4201

Oklahoma
4020 North Lincoln Blvd.
Oklahoma City, OK 73105
Phone: 405-424-4003

Oregon
220 Cottage Street N.E.
Salem, OR 97301
Phone: 503-581-1466

Pennsylvania
222 North Third Street
Harrisburg, PA 17101
Phone: 717-255-3252

Rhode Island
30 Exchange Terrace
Providence, RI 02903
Phone: 401-521-5000

South Carolina
1201 Main Street, #1810
Columbia, SC 29201-3229
Phone: 803-799-4601

South Dakota
Box 548
Pierre, SD 57501
Phone: 605-224-7361

Tennessee
161 4th Avenue N.
Nashville, TN 37219
Phone: 615-259-4755

Texas
Box 1967
Austin, TX 78767
Phone: 512-478-9383

Utah
175 East 400 S., #600
Salt Lake City, UT 84111
Phone: 801-364-3631

Vermont
134 State Street
Montpelier, VT 05602
Phone: 802-828-3236

Virginia
3600 Broad Street, 5th Floor
Richmond, VA 23230
Phone: 804-367-8500

Washington
Box 1427
1000 Plum Street
Olympia, WA 98507
Phone: 206-357-3362

West Virginia
Box 2789
Charleston, WV 25330
Phone: 304-342-1115

Wisconsin
756 N. Milwaukee Street
Milwaukee, WE 53202
Phone: 414-273-3000

Wyoming
Box 1147
Cheyenne, WY 82003
Phone: 307-638-3388

Bibliography

BARITZ, LOREN. *The Good Life.* New York: Harper & Row, 1982.

BLOOM, ALLAN. *The Closing of the American Mind.* New York: Simon and Schuster, 1987.

BOLLES, RICHARD. *What Color Is Your Parachute?* Berkeley: Ten Speed Press, 1990.

BOYER, RICHARD, and SAVAGEAU, DAVID. *Places Rated Almanac: Your Guide to Finding the Best Places to Live in America.* New York: Prentice Hall, 1989.

———. *Retirement Places Rated.* New York: Prentice Hall, 1987.

CAMPBELL, JOSEPH. *The Power of Myth.* New York: Doubleday, 1988.

FIELDS, RICK, et al. *Chop Wood, Carry Water.* Los Angeles: Jeremy Tarcher, 1984.

FULGHUM, ROBERT. *All I Really Need to Know I Learned in Kindergarten.* New York: Villard Books, 1986.

GAWAIN, SHAKTI. *Creative Visualization.* San Rafael, Ca.: New World Library, 1978.

GREGG, RICHARD. *The Value of Voluntary Simplicity.* Wallingford, Pa.: Pendle Hill, 1936.

HADFIELD, J. A. *The Psychology of Modern Problems.* Ayer & Co., 1973.

HAWKEN, PAUL. *Growing a Business.* New York: Simon and Schuster, 1987.

HILL, NAPOLEON. *Think and Grow Rich.* New York: Fawcett Crest, 1960.

HOLT, JOHN. *Never Too Late.* Pinchpenny Press, 1984.

JAMES, WILLIAM. *The Varieties of Religious Experience.* New York: Randon House, 1932.

KINDER, MELVYN. *Going Nowhere Fast.* New York: Prentice Hall Press, 1991.

KORN, LESTER. *The Success Profile.* New York: Simon and Schuster, 1988.

LESSINGER, JACK. *Regions of Opportunity.* New York: Times Books, 1986.

NEARING, HELEN AND SCOTT. *Living the Good Life.* New York: Schocken Books, 1970.

NOZICK, ROBERT. *The Examined Life.* New York: Simon and Schuster, 1989.

PEALE, NORMAN VINCENT. *The Power of Positive Thinking.* New York: Fawcett, 1978.

PHILLIPS, MICHAEL. *The Briarpatch Book.* New Glide/Reed, 1975.

ROSZAK, THEODORE. *The Making of a Counter Culture: Reflections on the Technocratic Society and Its Youthful Opposition.* Garden City, N.Y.: Doubleday, 1969.

———. *Where the Wasteland Ends: Politics and Transcendence in Post-Industrial Society.* New York: Doubleday, 1973.

SCHER, LES. *Finding and Buying Your Place in the Country.* New York: Macmillan Publishing, 1974.

SHAMES, LAURENCE. *The Hunger for More.* New York: Times Books, 1989.

SHI, DAVID E. *In Search of the Simple Life.* Salt Lake City: Peregrine Smith, 1986.

SIMONTON, DEAN. *Genius, Creativity and Leadership.* Harvard University Press, 1984.

SINETAR, MARSHA. *Do What You Love, The Money Will Follow.* New York: Dell Publishing, 1987.

SWAIN, MADELEINE AND ROBERT. *Out the Organization.* New York: Donald Fine Inc., 1989.

TENDZIN, OSEL. *Buddha in the Palm of Your Hand.* Boston: Shambhala Publications, 1982.

TERHORST, PAUL. *Cashing In on the American Dream.* New York: Bantam Books, 1988.

TULKU, TARTHANG. *Skillful Means.* Berkeley, Calif.: Dharma Publications, 1978.

WHYTE, WILLIAM H. *City.* New York: Doubleday, 1988.

About the Author

M. M. Kirsch was born in Rhinelander, Wisconsin. She has a degree in philosophy from Mount Holyoke College. She is the author of four nonfiction books and has appeared on more than 50 radio and television talk shows. She has lectured and worked with the American Cancer Society. For the past 13 years she has owned her own agency in Hollywood, representing commercial artists and photographers nationally. She and her husband are in the process of leaving their fast-track careers and, with their baby girl, moving to their farm in northern Wisconsin to live a simpler life.